The Civil War

Remembered

The Civil War Remembered

Carl Lowe

FRIEDMAN/FAIRFAX

PUBLISHERS

A FRIEDMAN/FAIRFAX BOOK

Library of Congress Cataloging-in-Publication Data

Lowe, Carl.
   The Civil war remembered / Carl Lowe.
      p.   cm.
   Includes bibliographical references (p.) and index.
   ISBN 1-56799-107-6 (pbk.)
   1. United States--History--Civil War, 1861-1865.   2. United
States--History--Civil War, 1861-1865--Pictorial works.   I. Title.
E468.L92   1994
973.7--dc20   94-8757
                                           CIP

Editor: Suzanne DeRouen
Art Direction: Devorah Levinrad
Designer: Kevin Ullrich
Photography Editor: Anne K. Price

Originally published as *Civil War Storyteller*

Typeset by Bookworks Plus
Printed and bound in China by L.Rex Printing Company Limited

Additional Photo Credit: p. 3 Courtesy of the Library of Congress

For bulk purchases and special sales, please contact:
Friedman/Fairfax Publishers
15 West 26th Street
New York, NY 10010
212/685-6610 FAX 212/685-1307

DEDICATION

To my mother

ACKNOWLEDGEMENTS

Thanks to Stephen Williams, Bob Hernandez, and Suzanne DeRouen for their help in putting this book together.

C O N T

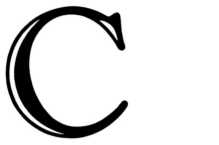

E N T S

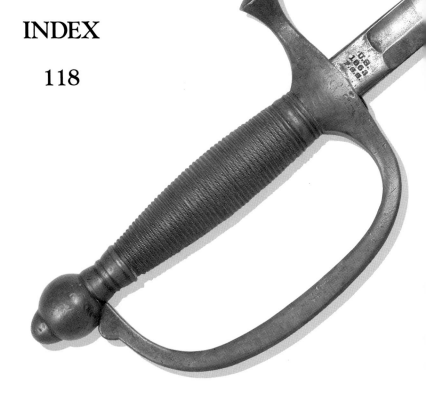

INTRODUCTION

Superficially, the American Civil War may seem a rather dry subject. The overall facts appear simple: two sections of the United States (North and South) disagreed about the future of the nation; two large armies were raised; battles were fought; and the more populous, prosperous group of states—the North—subdued the rebellious South.

But to those who study this period closely, the era hardly comes across as a conglomeration of individual events. The people of this era, caught in a momentous struggle called the Civil War, all had their own stories of how they were thrust into an epoch of death, destruction, and abrupt social upheaval. And each of these stories touched upon countless others.

Perhaps that is why the Civil War is particularly suited to be the setting for a storyteller—one who can tell of a people who entered a war as citizens of scattered states and came out of the conflict as citizens of a united country.

Civil War stories bring together people of very different backgrounds and show how this conflagration raged among groups of citizens who were more fragmented socially, economically, and spiritually than they would be ever again. These disparate groups, separated by geography; by ignorance of each other; and by conflicting ideas of how the country should be governed, violently confronted each other *en masse*.

The results of the confrontation were tragic and disheartening, and were often characterized by brutality. Yet the transition of the country and the stories of how individuals experienced this upheaval are fascinating. Country bump-kins acquainted with only the simplest technology stared point blank into the churning machines of modern warfare and their awesome killing power. African-Americans, who were considered second-class citizens (or worse), proved themselves to be gallant fighters. Through the use of audacious strategy, ragtag armies held their own against better-equipped, larger forces. Photography brought the realities of warfare home to civilians for the first time in American history. Railroads and telegraphs moved men and information at previously undreamed-of speed. And humans came face to face with widespread death on a frightening scale.

Many soldiers fighting in the Civil War sent pictures and locks of their hair to their loved ones as mementos (below). It was the first American war captured on film. This scene (far left) contrasts the orderly stacking of Union muskets along a Petersburg road with the war's devastation in the background.

9

By telling the story of the American Civil War through individual stories, this book aims not only to capture the flavor of the war as experienced by those who lived through it, but also to give a deeper understanding of the war's impact on the country's future.

Many of the underlying conflicts that resulted in this war are still present in the United States and other countries today—problems of equality among citizens and the question of how a large conglomeration of states can function as one country while doing justice to the individual states within the larger unit.

Religious questions also arise from the Civil War. There is the evident paradox of two warring parties who each claimed that an omnipotent God was on their side. Also, the sight of large armies of God-fearing, Bible-toting soldiers tearing each other apart inflamed the philosophical debate surrounding the metaphysics of morality. These are debates that continue to the present as the technology of warfare continually and unfortunately surpasses our understanding of the destructive potential of the weapons we have created.

Not only do these stories allow us to understand forces still at work today, they also give us a better sense of what made the United States a world power. It is only through individual stories, collectively forming the story of a nation, that a large, unruly, historic event like the American Civil War eventually seems to form a coherent whole.

At the time of the war, of course, observers and participants would have been hard pressed to understand how the smaller events in which they were involved contributed to the overall thrust of history. For those who lived through this war, the desperate immediacy of each frantic moment often concealed the overarching significance of the struggle.

Our perspective insulates us from the contemporary confusion that surrounded the noise and fury of the ongoing battles and clashes. By listening to the stories of this war, we can visualize the warring factions, the Blue versus the Gray, citizen versus citizen, and imagine what it was like to be there.

This war was one of the last to use wooden ships in combat. By the end of the conflict military men grasped the necessity of vessels with hulls of reinforced metal. This schooner was equipped with mortars that lobbed shells at the enemy.

chapter 1

SETTING THE STAGE FOR WAR

Southern mansions like these in Natchez, Missis- sippi, were monuments to a pre–Civil War social order that depended on slavery.

The Southern economy depended on the cotton crop that was cleaned of seeds by the cotton gin, invented by Eli Whitney (right). This agrarian economic system couldn't match the war effort mounted by the North, which was home to many factories like this one in Waterfield, Massachusetts.

The power struggle that led to the Civil War stemmed largely from the fact that the two sections of the United States, the North and South, evolved quite differently after the creation of the country. And to this very day, North and South remain distinctly different, in part because of the Civil War, among other differing factors.

In the period immediately following the Revolutionary War, the United States population, both North and South, consisted almost entirely of farmers. But as urban areas expanded during the early 1800s, and the machinery of the Industrial Revolution began to make its presence felt, the Northern population grew, adapted to technology, and embraced an industrialized social order more rapidly than the more conservative South.

That the geographic unevenness of these changes resulted in war was primarily due to the divisive issue of slavery. The modernizing economy of the North left no room for this antiquated, morally repugnant form of labor. In a sense, the Industrial Revolution was the beginning of the era when machines would increasingly become the only slave that society would need—replacing animal and human labor.

The South's hot climate and more rigid agrarian social structure, dominated by rich plantation owners, was at least partly to blame for its leisurely resistance to increases in industrial capacity. The South clung to its right to slavery. Its ruling class considered the enslavement of blacks as an economic necessity, which it viewed as threatened by the power-hungry North.

Ironically, the social and technological changes that the United States experienced between 1800 and 1860 not only helped motivate the South to secede from the Union and initiate the hostilities marking the beginning of the Civil War, but these very same circumstances also ensured that the Confederacy would face virtually insurmountable odds in pursuing a war against the Northern states. During the war, industrialization enabled the North to create a war machine that proved unbeatable. The South had unwittingly dug its own grave from the beginning.

ELI WHITNEY— INVENTOR AT HISTORY'S CROSSROADS

Astride the long list of ironies inherent in the Civil War stands Eli Whitney, inventor of the cotton gin—a simple machine designed to separate cotton from its seeds, hulls, and foreign material. Some historians speculate that without this invention, the processing of cotton would have become so uneconomical that, by the 1850s, cotton growing and, consequently, slavery, which primarily existed to harvest cotton, would have declined in the South to such a degree that the Civil War might never have occurred.

Eli Whitney, the savior of "King Cotton," was a Yankee tinkerer born in Westborough, Massachusetts, in 1765. As a child, during the Revolutionary War, he made and sold nails, a commodity hard to come by in those primitive

days. At age twenty-seven, after a protracted and sporadic college career, he graduated from Yale, his tinkering days supposedly over.

From Yale he went on down to Savannah, Georgia, in pursuit of a teaching job. But on arriving, the inveterate inventor became intrigued by local complaints that there was no machine designed to remove cotton seeds from the fiber. The most commonly grown kind of cotton was difficult to clean by hand, lowering its value.

Whitney only needed about a week and a half to conceptually solve this problem and come up with the basic design for the "gin" (short for engine)—a device that pulled the cotton through a screen, separating it from the seeds. However, Whitney originally made little or no money from his invention, as thousands of farmers freely stole his idea. He

patented the process in 1793, and sixteen years later finally won the lawsuits that allowed him to make money from his invention.

Unfortunately for the plantation owners, Whitney's genius not only boosted the South's economy but it eventually helped seal its doom as well. The cotton gin made slavery a more economic mode of production. A greater number of slaves were now available to pick more cotton to be processed by the new machine. Slavery, therefore, became even more deeply entrenched in the South's productive infrastructure.

Beginning in 1798, back in New Haven, Connecticut, Whitney entered into the defense-contracting business when he agreed to make ten thousand muskets for the U.S. Government. Production, however, ran late and into cost over-

Soon after Whitney invented the cotton gin, the machine was in wide use throughout the Southern states.

THE COTTON GIN.

runs. Instead of delivering all the guns in 1800—as the contract stipulated—Whitney finally delivered the last musket in 1809.

But Whitney's great contribution to the North's weapon-manufacturing capacity was something he referred to as a "uniformity system." Under this system, factory machines cranked out interchangeable components, which could be installed in any of the manufactured guns without extra, customizing work being done by hand. Some experts argue that Whitney stole this idea from the French. But original or not, it was Whitney's company that established assembly line weapons manufacturing in the United States. As a result, at the time of the Civil War, it was the North's efficient armament factories that produced the overwhelming firepower that helped crush the secession.

"BLEEDING KANSAS"

Even before formal fighting between North and South began in 1861 at Fort Sumter, South Carolina, pro- and anti-slavery forces had been battling in the Kansas territory since 1854. The fight was over whether or not slavery would be allowed in Kansas. Up until this date, the Missouri Compromise of 1820 stood. The compromise decreed that all new states admitted to the Union south of the Missouri River would be designated slave states, while those north of the river would prohibit slavery altogether. In that year, Congress imprudently passed the Kansas-Nebraska Act, negating the old compromise and mandating plebiscites to decide the slavery issue in the new western territories. Whether or not these newly developed territories of

Horace Greeley was one of many Northern journalists whose editorials inflamed abolitionist emotions in the North.

the west would become slave or free states was to be decided by a vote of the residents.

Abolitionists (those in favor of abolishing slavery) from the Northeast migrated to Kansas to increase the anti-slavery vote. At the same time, from Missouri, the state adjacent to the eastern border of the territory, pro-slavery citizens flooded into the area to vote against, and eventually to fight, the abolitionists.

While men like Horace Greeley, the abolitionist editor of the *New York Herald Tribune*, told Northeasterners, "Go west, young man" (women, who couldn't vote, were encouraged to stay home), others, like New Englander Eli Thayer, started the Massachusetts Emigrant Aid Company, the purpose of which was to send money and arms to the anti-slavery forces.

The Reverend Henry Ward Beecher, a Brooklyn abolitionist, surmised in a widely read sermon that, in Kansas, there was more moral force in a rifle than in a Bible. When his organization was accused of using boxes meant for Bibles for smuggling rifles to Kansas, abolitionists' rifles became known as "Beecher's Bibles." (In 1852, Beecher's sister, Harriet Beecher Stowe, wrote *Uncle Tom's Cabin*, an anti-slavery book that raised the ire of Northerners.)

Missourians viewed the Northerners' intrusion with alarm. One wrote, "We are threatened . . . with the filth, scum, and offscourings of the East . . . to preach abolitionism and dig underground railroads."

From the conflict in Kansas and the rest of the country, the political party known as the Republican party was born as part of the effort to make the western territories anti-slavery. Until this time, the two main U.S. parties had been the Whigs and the Democrats. While, for a variety of reasons, the Democrats largely turned into a pro-slavery organization, the weakening Whig party eventually disbanded and many former members joined the anti-slavery Republican party.

The political change was chaotic. Politicians in Illinois were apparently some of the first to adopt the new name "Republican" for their organization. In 1854, when they approached a young lawyer named Abraham Lincoln and

The Reverend Henry Ward Beecher preached the use of force to halt the spread of slavery. Abolitionist rifles shipped to Kansas became known as "Beecher's Bibles."

asked him to be on their central committee, he turned them down and decided to run for the state legislature on the Whig ticket. It wasn't until after this campaign that he became a Republican.

In 1856, the prewar violence in Kansas reached its height. On May 21 of that year, pro-slavery forces under the direction of Sheriff Samuel Jones "sacked" the town of Lawrence, Kansas, the headquarters of the anti-slavery forces. Actually, the attacking forces did little more than toss a couple of abolitionist printing presses into a local river, consume the town's supply of whiskey, and burn one building. Despite the minimal damage caused, abolitionist newspapers inflated the event as though it were a significant atrocity.

The only human casualty of this incident was a member of the pro-slavery attacking forces, who was killed when a piece of a burning building fell on him. But any chance for peaceful coexistence between the abolitionists and the

John Brown Takes Up Arms

John Brown (inset, right) led a raid on Harper's Ferry, Virginia (right), that was meant to stir up a slaves' rebellion. But all it stirred was the Southerner's fear of abolitionists.

Born in 1800 in Torrington, Connecticut, John Brown, a self-righteous fanatic, was one of the more violent partakers in the carnage of "Bleeding Kansas." Many historians consider him to have been a lunatic. At the trial, where he was eventually condemned to death by hanging, seventeen affidavits alluding to his insanity were filed by his friends and neighbors. (Brown once flogged his four-year-old son because the boy "lied" about a dream he had.)

Until he became a fanatic revolutionary devoted to killing pro-slavers, Brown's life consisted of one financial disaster after another. While trying to support a family that included twenty children, twelve of whom grew to maturity, he failed as a farmer, land speculator, tanner, sheep rancher, and surveyor. He managed to fail at more than twenty business ventures in six states. Although he owed money wherever he established residence, he was never known to have stolen a penny while engaging in anti-slavery activities.

On the night of May 24, 1856, after the sacking of Lawrence, Kansas, Brown, along with four of his sons, a son-in-law, and a few others went door-to-door at Dutch Henry's Crossing at Pottawatomie Creek, called five men out of bed, and hacked them to death with broad swords, shot one of them for good measure and cut off a hand from the corpses. The exact motive for what became known as the Pottawatomie Massacre is and probably will always be unknown. While the executions might have been revenge for what happened at Lawrence, it is believed by some that these deaths were simply a Kansas version of a "mob hit"—some of the victims were allegedly supposed to testify against Brown and others in a court case.

Whatever Brown's motives were at Pottawatomie, the results were predictable. The massacre helped inspire other violent acts of vengence by both pro- and anti-slavery groups.

John Brown's ultimate moment of glory occurred at Harper's Ferry, Virginia, where he began what was meant to be a bloody slave's rebellion against their Southern masters. On October 16, 1859, Brown, along with five African-Americans and about twenty white men, took over the United States arsenal at Harper's Ferry. Brown's plan was to seize rifles and arms to supply slaves for their insurrection.

U.S. Marines, led by Robert E. Lee and James Ewell Brown "Jeb" Stuart, both of whom were later to be important Confederate commanders, captured Brown after ten of his men, including two of his sons, were killed or wounded. In the battle, four marines were also killed and nine were wounded. Brown, too, would have been killed in the battle, but the soldier who injured him used a dress sword, a comparatively blunt weapon.

Brown's raid on Harper's Ferry undoubtedly hastened the beginning of the war. The venture scared Southerners who accused Republican abolitionists of subsidizing Brown's adventure, which was true. Northern abolitionists considered Brown a hero, and used his name as a rallying cry against slavery.

On December 2, 1859, Brown was hanged. He disappointed everyone by remaining silent in the moments before his execution. Spectators had hoped for a long, dramatic speech like the one he gave at his trial. His final words, in a note given to his jailer, were: "I, John Brown, am now quite *certain* that the crimes of this *guilty* land will never be purged *away* but with blood."

pro-slavers was also a casualty of the skirmish. In the following months more than two hundred people were killed during clashes in what was to be called "Bleeding Kansas."

THE RISING TIDE OF VIOLENCE

The violence in Kansas was symptomatic of a rising level of hostility in the relations between the North and South, which even reached into the Senate. In Washington, DC, the day after the sacking of Lawrence, Representative Preston Brooks of South Carolina paid a visit to the Senate chamber to confront Senator Charles Sumner of Massachusetts about the senator's long oration entitled, "The Crime Against Kansas."

Sumner was known for using the Senate floor as a soapbox for vituperative attacks on the South and pro-slavery politicians. But his pièce de résistance speech had been particularly nasty, calling Missourians the "vomit of an uneasy civilization," and attacking Senator Andrew Butler of South Carolina not only for being "polluted in the sight of the world," but also for his "loose expectoration" (he often spit saliva while he spoke).

Brooks, who was related to Butler, was so outraged by these insults that he beat Sumner with his cane until it shattered and other legislators restrained him.

Because of his injuries, Sumner didn't return to the Senate floor for two and half years, although his detractors said that he was just faking. As a result of these violent confrontations, other legislators began arming themselves with guns and knives. Psychologically, they were preparing themselves for a real war.

PREWAR POLITICAL CHAOS

As a young lawyer from Illinois, Abraham Lincoln was a typically loyal member of the Whig party. It wasn't until the turmoil in the western territories had reached fever pitch that he felt the need to join the new Republican party and actively oppose slavery (at the same time, the Whig party was also being torn to pieces by dissension over the slavery issue). His original stand on slavery was that there was no need to actually ban it. In his view, if this "peculiar institution," as it had been dubbed, were restricted to the existing slave states and not allowed in any new states that might join the Union, eventually slavery would cease to exist altogether.

At the time of the Kansas-Nebraska Act of 1854, neither of the two existing political parties was prepared to deal with slavery as a fundamental issue. Both the Whigs and the Democrats contained pro- and anti-slavery factions. On other political fronts, the Whigs were generally in favor of protecting property values. The Democrats were more of a populist party. But in order to keep their influence in both the North and South, neither group was ready to take a firm stand on slavery.

New parties sprang up to take advantage of the strong feelings about slavery. For a while, an anti-slavery party called the Free Soil party enjoyed success in New York, Massachusetts, and Vermont. At the same time, a group called the Barnburners gathered strength in New York. The Liberty party came and went as did the Fusion party, Anti-Nebraska party, Know-Nothings, Know-Somethings, Hard-Shell Democrats, Soft-Shells, Half-Shells, and so on. At one point, the Know-Nothing party splintered into the North Americans and the South Americans.

As a result of these shifting political alliances, in the presidential campaign of 1856 there were three candidates nominated by five different parties: John C. Freemont, running as a Republican and a North American Know-Nothing; Millard Fillmore, as a Whig and a South American Know-Nothing; and John Buchanan, who ran at the head of the Democratic ticket.

When the dust settled, the 1856 presidential election marked the end of the Whig party. Anti-slavery politicians, like Lincoln, ended up as Republicans, while the pro-slavery groups migrated to the Democrats.

War correspondents followed the troops and filed dispatches to a public hungry for news of the conflict. Here, reporters for the New York Herald *sit beside their field headquarters at Bealoton, Virginia, in the summer of 1863.*

Media Wars

The Civil War period represents for the first time in the history of all wars that the media—which consisted at the time solely of widely circulated newspapers—played an influential role in swaying the hearts and minds of the people who weren't engaged on the battlefield. The phrase "Bleeding Kansas" was created and exploited by abolitionist editors like Horace Greeley. Another paper, the *National Era*, was so biased against the people of Missouri and the pro-slavery factions that it employed as its Kansas correspondent John Kagi, a man who had shot a pro-slavery territorial judge.

When Sam Jones and his men marched into Lawrence and burned just one building, the *Tribune* reported the incident with a large, sensational, and, for the most part, false headline: "Lawrence in Ruins—Several Persons Slaughtered." The *New York Times* printed similar hysteria. When the truth came out about a week later, both papers printed retractions—in much smaller, less conspicuous print.

But when John Brown and his men cold-bloodedly hacked bleary-eyed Kansans to death at Pottawatomie, the *Times* discounted the slaughter as being "improbable," despite eyewitness accounts. The *Tribune* claimed that the mutilations were obviously evidence that Comanche Indians were the true killers—an absurd accusation.

Southerners considered Abraham Lincoln (opposite page) a "black Republican" dedicated to the abolition of slavery. Soon after his election to the presidency, Southern states began to secede from the Union, and the North was mustering troops en masse (right) to put down the rebellion.

LINCOLN'S CANDIDACY MEANS WAR

The final event that led to the secession of the southern states and the Civil War was the election of Abraham Lincoln as the sixteenth president of the United States. When Southerners realized that Republicans—essentially a party of Northerners organized to oppose slavery—would control the White House, they decided that no reconciliation with the North was possible.

But who was Abraham Lincoln? He was one of the most enigmatic figures ever to enter and dominate American politics. He told homespun, folksy jokes that his more refined acquaintances considered to be in bad taste. But, on the other hand, he could reason and debate with the most sophisticated political thinkers. Although usually secretive about his emotions and naturally reclusive (among his friends he was known as a quiet and moody character, given to deep depressions), he could, as a public speaker, effortlessly reveal his most deeply held personal beliefs with a mix of personality and facility with words that gave him convincing political charisma.

Tall and bony as a young man, he had a reputation as a successful athlete, winning local acclaim by outwrestling the competition in Illinois. Largely uneducated as a youth, he managed to study and become a successful lawyer. His frontier upbringing made him a strong potential candidate. His publicists found it easy to create the popular image of "Honest Abe," the former rail splitter. Among the voters, the lanky politician proved to be a most popular choice.

Lincoln's Republican nomination for the Senate in 1858 against Stephen Douglas vaulted him into national attention. The two of them—a physically mismatched pair, with Lincoln standing six feet four inches and Douglas more than a foot shorter—held a series of seven debates across Illinois wherein Lincoln argued that slavery should not be allowed in new states. Douglas held that new territories should decide the slavery issue for themselves.

Douglas won the election to the Senate even though Lincoln got more votes. In those days, the state legislature, controlled by Douglas's Democratic allies, had the final decision over who went to Washington. But the election had long-range consequences for both men. For Douglas, the fact that he didn't favor slavery even more strongly— many Southerners believed that citizens of the new territories should have to accept slavery without say in the matter—cost him the Southern support for a successful Democratic presidential candidacy.

Lincoln realized that he had benefited from the race because, even though he lost, the campaign gave him a chance to address "the great and durable question of the age": slavery. After the state legislature confirmed Douglas as senator, Lincoln added, perhaps with wry humor, "I now sink out of view, and shall be forgotten, (although) I believe I have made some marks which will tell for the cause of civil liberty."

After Lincoln's defeat in the Senate, he continued to travel widely, making speeches. A particularly well-received talk was given at Cooper Union in New York City on February 27, 1860. This event is generally credited with cementing his position in the forefront of Republican national leadership. On May 16, 1860, he won the Republican nomination for president on the third ballot at the convention in Chicago, Illinois.

chapter 2

THE BATTLE BEGINS

Northern soldiers who survived the war received certificates and the Stars and Stripes. This flag and document were awarded to James L. Talmadge (pictured with his wife), who served in Company B, 27th Infantry of New Jersey. Today, many of the battlefields on which these soldiers fought (Antietam, opposite page) have been preserved in dedication to those who risked or lost their lives there.

When South Carolina became the first state to secede, the **Charleston Mercury** *trumpeted the news in this extra edition.*

Indications that the South would truly secede if Lincoln was elected were initially ridiculed by Northerners. The threat was called the "old game," and the "old mumbo-jumbo." One Northerner recalled that Southern congressmen had once walked out of the House of Representatives in protest about a slavery issue. But, he said, after they had had a drink, they came back. If Lincoln were elected they would have two drinks and come back.

The American poet and editor William Cullen Bryant said, "As to disunion, nobody but silly people expect it will happen."

But the silly people were proved right. After Lincoln was elected president, seven southern states, convinced that with a "Black Republican" as president their sovereignty as slave states would be threatened, declared their independence from the United States and seceded.

On December 20, 1860, South Carolina became the first southern state to withdraw from the United States. On January 9, 1861, Mississippi followed suit. In quick succession, Alabama, Georgia, and Louisiana seceded. By the time Lincoln set off from his home in Springfield, Illinois, on February 11, 1860, for his inauguration, seven states (with the addition of Florida and Texas)—all in the Deep South—had quit the Union and formed the Confederate States of America.

In the face of this crisis, Lincoln and his advisors hesitated to use force to coerce these states back into the Union, thinking that some sort of compromise or negotiation would end the secession. On the other hand, the slave states that were not very far from the North, such as Virginia, were not eager to secede since they had the strongest economic ties to the North. They also had much fewer slaves than the states of the Deep South and they felt they had the most to lose from a war between the Union and a new nation of southern states.

When South Carolinians fired on Federal troops stationed in Fort Sumter on April 12, 1861, it was not just a show of force against the Union. It was a move designed to force the other slave states to secede and join the newly

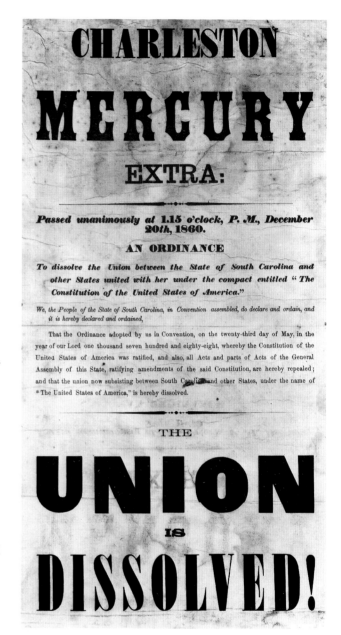

CHARLESTON MERCURY

EXTRA:

Passed unanimously at 1.15 o'clock, P. M., December 20th, 1860.

AN ORDINANCE

To dissolve the Union between the State of South Carolina and other States united with her under the compact entitled "The Constitution of the United States of America."

We, the People of the State of South Carolina, in Convention assembled, do declare and ordain, and it is hereby declared and ordained,

That the Ordinance adopted by us in Convention, on the twenty-third day of May, in the year of our Lord one thousand seven hundred and eighty-eight, whereby the Constitution of the United States of America was ratified, and also, all Acts and parts of Acts of the General Assembly of this State, ratifying amendments of the said Constitution, are hereby repealed; and that the union now subsisting between South Carolina and other States, under the name of "The United States of America," is hereby dissolved.

THE UNION IS DISSOLVED!

formed Confederate States. The South Carolinians, who seemed to be the most eager secessionists, knew that when the bullets started flying, Washington would have to ask all the states to provide troops to fight the rebellion. They also knew that Virginia and the other southern states who had not yet seceded would never agree to this request.

As predicted, the day after the shelling began at Fort Sumter, Lincoln asked for troops from all the states. Immediately, Virginia, North Carolina, Arkansas, and Tennessee left the Union. Rather than supply militia to the Federal government to fight fellow Southerners, these states began mustering troops to aid the secession. Up until this time, the capital of the Confederacy had been Montgomery, Alabama. Now it moved to Richmond, Virginia.

THE SHOOTING STARTS AT FORT SUMTER

In the spring of 1861, neither the Confederacy nor the Federal government was adequately prepared for the long war that was about to begin. The United States only had seventeen thousand soldiers in uniform. The Confederate states had poorly organized state militias.

Fort Sumter in Charleston Harbor, South Carolina, where the Confederacy first confronted the Union, was unfinished, although it was well fortified. In April 1861, under the command of Major Robert Anderson, the fort contained only 125 men, forty of whom were workmen still completing the fortifications. Anderson was surrounded by smaller forts manned by hostile South Carolinians on surrounding islands. The mainland also bristled with artillery pointing in his direction. He was under siege and the Southerners were waiting for him to run out of food and water.

Ironically, the forces opposing Anderson were under the command of a brigadier general with the rather impressive name of Pierre G. T. Beauregard, who two decades earlier had learned his artillery skills at West Point under the tutelage of Anderson. Anderson himself, who was about to

become the first commander of Union troops under fire, was from Kentucky, where he had formerly owned slaves. Both Beauregard and Anderson had served and been wounded in the Mexican War.

Before dawn on April 12, 1861, the Confederates, who were tired of waiting for Anderson to surrender and afraid that Union reinforcements might be on their way, opened fire on Fort Sumter. For thirty-six hours, the two sides exchanged artillery shells without casualty on either side.

Jefferson Davis was inaugurated as president of the Confederacy in Montgomery, Alabama. After the war began, the capital moved to Richmond, Virginia—much more difficult to defend against Union attack.

In April 1861, Union Major Robert Anderson (inset, right) surrendered Fort Sumter to Pierre G. T. Beauregard, a Confederate soldier who had been Anderson's pupil at West Point twenty years earlier.

The citizens of Charlestown stood on rooftops watching the noisy but ineffectual display of armaments.

Mary Boykin Chestnut, wife of James Chestnut, a former congressman and now advisor to Jefferson Davis, wrote in her diary, "Boom, boom goes the cannon all the time. I did not know that one could endure such days of excitement."

Unfortunately for both the North and South, no other battles would be casualty-free as Fort Sumter was. On the evening of April 13, Anderson, running short of ammunition and with several of the fort's buildings on fire, was forced to surrender. As second-in-command Captain Abner Doubleday reported, "The roaring and crackling of the flames, the dense masses of whirling smoke, the bursting of the enemy's shells and our own, which were exploding in the burning rooms, the crashing of the shot, and the sound of masonry falling in every direction made the fort a pandemonium."

After Anderson surrendered, the Confederates allowed him to fire a one-hundred-gun salute. But it was shortened to fifty when one of the guns exploded, killing Private Daniel Hough instantly. Ironically, after the Federals had withstood more than three thousand shells without losing a man, the first death of the war was from an accident while saluting the surrender of the fort.

THE BATTLE OF BULL RUN

Believing that slaves would turn against their Southern masters, most Northerners thought the war would be quickly and easily won. Initial enlistments in the Union army were only supposed to last three months. These three-month soldiers took part in small-scale skirmishes between the Northern and Southern armies during the early summer of 1861. In one of these battles—the Battle of Rich Mountain in western Virginia—the Northern press played up the heroism of General George Brinton McClellan. Whether or not McClellan deserved his newly found adulation is debat-

Although no one was killed in the initial shelling, Fort Sumter (left) was practically reduced to rubble in the opening conflict of the war.

Before the war began, soldiers on both sides thought it would end quickly and painlessly. These Confederates, the "Richmond Grays," are shown clowning for the camera before the first Battle of Bull Run.

able, but the papers were anxious for heroes and not much else was going on. He would do until the next champion came along.

The first serious confrontation between military forces was destined to occur at Bull Run, a stream located near Manassas, Virginia, a town about twenty-five miles southwest of Washington, DC. (During the war the North referred to battles by the names of nearby waterways. The South preferred to use the names of towns.)

In the second week of July 1861, both sides gathered their forces at their respective capital cities—Washington and Richmond—which were only a hundred miles apart. Lincoln, anxious for a victory, urged General Irvin McDowell, his top field commander, to make an aggressive move south. The Confederate Congress was scheduled to meet on July 20 in Richmond, and Northerners clamored for a decisive military victory before then.

The Confederate commander responsible for defending Richmond was Brigadier General Pierre Beauregard, the man who had captured Fort Sumter. He and McDowell had been classmates at West Point.

The amateurish Union troops treated the march from Washington toward Manassas as a bit of a lark, still fully expecting that the war would be quick and easy. They displayed a lack of discipline that would later spell disaster when they faced the Confederates.

They stopped every moment "to pick blackberries or get water," McDowell said. "They were not used to denying themselves much." Their inexperience would help deny them the victory they thought would be so effortless.

Because of the delays, the march proceeded at the rate of barely six miles a day, half as quickly as would later be expected of the Union army when the war was fully under way. As they marched they foraged for food throughout the countryside. An army nurse reported, "The whole neighborhood was ransacked for milk, butter, eggs, poultry . . . . Stray shots (were) fired in the direction of a field where a drove of cattle were quietly grazing. . . ."

Well-versed in drills and military formations practiced in camps around Washington, D.C. (above), Union troops would prove at Bull Run in July 1861 that they still had a lot to learn about winning battles.

Youngsters in their early teens joined up with both sides in the war. Most, like Gilbert A. Marbury of the New York 22nd (above), served as drummer boys.

The Federal troops didn't bother to consider that they were marching through enemy territory and that the local citizens were keeping the Confederates well-informed of their movements. If the Union army had kept as aware of the Confederate movements, perhaps they could have avoided the debacle that followed.

But even as McDowell marched south to challenge Beauregard, other forces confronted each other in the Shenandoah Valley. There, about fifty miles from Manassas, Union General Robert Patterson was under orders to keep the forces of Confederate General Joseph J. Johnston engaged so that they would stay clear of Bull Run.

Despite his lack of intelligence reports, McDowell's initial battle plan for fighting at Bull Run was well-conceived and should have worked. At the onset of battle, McDowell's thirty-five thousand men lined up against a roughly equal force of about thirty-three thousand rebels. Despite the fact that most of the men who should have been pinned down by Patterson had secretly slipped away and actually joined Beauregard's troops, McDowell still had slightly more troops in the field.

On the morning of July 21, the Union forces prepared to make a diversionary, small-scale attack on the Confederate center, while the real attack would take place against the relatively weak Confederate left flank. But the unseasoned Union troops weren't in position until nearly ten o'clock. That gave the Confederates enough time to figure out what was really going on—they could see the dust clouds raised on the road by the approaching army—and the rebels moved in reinforcements to meet the attack on their left flank.

Still, once the shooting started, the initial events favored the North. The rebel flank retreated just as McDowell had planned. The Union army advanced on a farm owned by an old woman named Judith Henry who was bedridden as the battle took place. The retreating Confederates used her house for cover while Union soldiers tore it apart, making her one of the first civilian casualties of the war.

At one point in the battle, General Bernard Bee of South Carolina, riding back and forth, trying to rally his troops, pointed to Thomas J. Jackson and his men. In a voice which rivalled the roar of battle, he cried out, "Oh, men, there are Jackson and his Virginians standing behind you like a stone wall!" Bee was killed by a Union bullet moments later, but the nickname stuck. Forever after, Jackson was known as "Stonewall" Jackson.

At around two o'clock, the Union army made its first serious error—in its haste to advance, it stationed important artillery batteries too close to a relatively unprotected section of its front lines. Soon after, a Confederate regiment came in swiftly and killed the artillerymen in a surprise move so abrupt that the cannoneers died with their rammers (sticks used to load the guns) still in their hands.

Despite this setback, by about four in the afternoon, both armies were tired and spent. It was at this moment that new Confederate reinforcements, who also were supposed to be pinned down by Patterson's men, arrived by train.

The result was disaster for the North. A more experienced force might have held the field, or perhaps only have made a small retreat. But these men had just made the first long march of their lives, had just fought their first serious battle, and were exhausted from what they presumptuously thought would be their first victory. The fresh Confederates easily sent the Northerners running in disorganized, uncontrolled flight. As McDowell said, the mad rush to escape the Confederate guns "soon degenerated into disorder for which there was no remedy."

At the battle, ready to publicize what they thought was to be a great Union victory, were correspondents for many Northern newspapers, as well as several congressmen. What they witnessed was an embarrassing loss. According to Edmund Stedman, reporter for the *New York World*, some of the congressmen displayed greater courage than many of the novice soldiers. "These congressmen bravely stood their ground till the last moment . . . (As for the troops) whoever saw such a flight?"

While the march down from Washington had taken a leisurely two and a half days, many of the soldiers high-tailed it back to the capital in less than eight hours. In their wake they left behind a long trail of discarded equipment.

It was at the Battle of Bull Run that Thomas J. Jackson (left) acquired the nickname "Stonewall" for his unwavering ferocity during battle.

Many of the first Union volunteers (right) only signed on for three-month enlistments. It was soon evident that the conflict was going to last much longer than that.

Instant Communication Spreads the War News

A part of what made the Civil War different from previous wars was the telegraph. In the past, news could only travel as fast as messengers on horseback, on ship, or on foot could deliver it. But almost as soon as the shelling of Fort Sumter began, news of the battle flashed across the country. Mary Ashton Livermore, who was later to work for the Union's war hospitals, reported that the telegraph "registered for the astounded nation the hourly progress of the bombardment, announced the lowering of the Stars and Stripes and the surrender of the beleaguered garrison."

Although the South certainly had telegraph facilities, the North held a significant advantage. Not only could Northern newspapers generally get news faster because of better and more extensive telegraph facilities, Union field commanders could communicate with headquarters more effectively. The North had access to as much supply of wire and portable telegraph posts as it needed. On the other hand, any telegraph wire the South needed had to be captured from the North, or imported from Europe and run through the Northern naval blockades.

The Union's telegraph facilities far outstripped the Confederates' capabilities. From Union field battery wagons (left), news flashed back almost instantaneously to Washington.

One paper reported, "Every impediment to flight was cast aside. Rifles, bayonets, pistols, haversacks, cartridge-boxes, canteens, blankets, belts, and overcoats lined the road." The Confederacy probably could have outfitted half its army with what the Union left behind.

At that moment, if the strong Confederate troops had marched on Washington, they might have been able to capture the city virtually unimpeded. But a day after the battle, heavy rains descended, turning the local roads into impassable mud.

After the battle, the South rejoiced, thinking that the future was assured, that the Confederacy could successfully beat back the North and retain independence. Jefferson Davis, who had witnessed part of the battle, reported back to the Confederate Congress in Richmond that the victory would cause European nations to recognize the Confederacy as a separate country from the United States. And even though the Southerners had lost two thousand men in the battle (the Union had three thousand killed, wounded, and missing in action), Confederates began to brag that "each Confederate soldier is worth five Yanks."

Instead of giving in to euphoria after Bull Run, the Confederates should have been paying more attention to how the North reacted to this defeat. Rather than making the North give up, this ugly defeat led the Union to redouble its resolve. The House of Representatives passed a unanimous resolution pledging the resources of Northern states "for the suppression, overthrow, and punishment of rebels in arms." And soon they'd be ready to put their bullets where they counted—into Confederate flesh.

Soldiers who carried the colors into battle were marked men as the opposition often took aim at them. This regimental flank marker of the 16th New York was carried into the Battle of Crampton's Pass by Corporal Charles H. Conant, who was promptly dispatched by a Confederate bullet that shattered his skull.

STONEWALL JACKSON— MILITARY MAN AND FOLK HERO

The tales told about Stonewall Jackson, legendary Southern general, reveal that in a war he was the kind of person you'd want fighting on your side.

Fearless in battle, unafraid of death, he thought that he was destined by God for great heroics. Events proved him right. He was a self-made man who was a bit of a misfit, the butt of jokes, and incredibly shy. Despite his disadvantages, his chance at fighting in the Civil War and being nicknamed by a fellow Confederate general made him a folk hero.

Born in Clarksburg, Virginia, in 1824, Jackson was orphaned when he was six years old, and he was raised by his uncle. He made the waiting list at West Point and was accepted when the student ahead of him resigned. After graduating, he fought in the Mexican War, but eventually his military career with the U.S. Army ended after he had a severe disagreement with a post commander.

Jackson became an artillery instructor and professor of natural philosophy at the Virginia Military Institute (VMI). At VMI, because of his strange, remarkably introverted manner, he was the target of many student pranks, derisive poems, and was even attacked by the Society of Alumni. However, when the Civil War started, and Virginia seceded the day after Fort Sumter was fired upon, Jackson marched the VMI cadets to Richmond and secured a commission as a colonel in the Virginia militia.

As a military tactician, Jackson was usually reliable and aggressive, although he was not always well liked by his men because of his egocentric and reserved ways. As a soldier on the move, his one physical flaw was an insatiable need for sleep. If he was disturbed at all during the night, he often fell fast asleep in the saddle the next day. Fellow officers reported hanging on to his coattails to keep the napping Jackson from falling off the saddle. His erratic behavior during one military campaign, where he made

Two weeks before being killed by Confederate friendly fire at Chancellorsville, Stonewall Jackson posed for this picture. While Chancellorsville was a smashing Southern victory, the loss of Jackson in the spring of 1863 hampered their military efforts during the rest of the war.

several tactical errors, was blamed on his staying up past his bedtime several nights in a row.

His belief in his own divine destiny alienated many of his fellow soldiers. Under fire, Jackson would stand fearlessly as men around him were shot to pieces. He was sure that he was invulnerable because God was on his side.

On the other hand, when battles were lost he had a disturbing tendency to blame the errors and mishaps on those around him. And when battles were won, instead of praising those who had done the hard fighting, he often reserved the credit for "Almighty God." His subordinates found this kind of reasoning disheartening.

Jackson's demise came at what should have been his finest hour. At Chancellorsville, Virginia, in May of 1863, he and Robert E. Lee were skillfully maneuvering their forces in an effort to outflank and defeat the army of Union General Joseph Hooker. At dawn on May 2, scouts reported

Contrabands

Although the Civil War did not witness bloody insurrections by slaves as John Brown expected and some Southerners feared, the hostilities did entice many slaves to run away from their masters and go north. Others left their homes and simply offered themselves for service to the Union army. For the Federal government, the problem of what to do with these runaways was a thorny political problem. Many Northerners, especially the abolitionists, favored declaring these slaves free men and women. But Lincoln did not want to alienate the border states that remained loyal to the Union but still permitted slavery—Missouri, Kentucky, Delaware, and Maryland.

Step by clumsy step, the Union stumbled toward freeing the slaves. At first the government merely allowed all fugitive slaves from secessionist states to remain free. Then it prevented the army from pursuing any fugitive slaves—even those who belonged to slave owners living in states that had not seceded.

In the meantime, the U.S. military was faced with the problem of what to do with the burgeoning crowd of fugitive African-Americans who constantly sought refuge behind Union lines. In May 1861, General Benjamin Butler, at Fort Monroe, Virginia, although under orders to return fugitive slaves, refused to do so. He knew that the slaves who were streaming into his camp had been used to build Confederate defense installations. As a rationale for retaining these people, he issued an order stating that they were "contraband"—property of the enemy that ought to be confiscated.

That was the birth of another nickname. For the rest of the war, runaway slaves were known as "contrabands."

At the opening of the war, Union generals were ordered to return escaped slaves to their masters. The generals soon refused, and used the refugees, nicknamed "contrabands," as laborers and teamsters (right).

a roundabout route that would take Jackson and his twenty-eight thousand men into a position to make a devastating attack from behind the Federal lines. By making what has been called one of the most remarkable marches in military history, Jackson took his men fifteen miles in less than a day before Hooker could fully counter-position his troops properly. (Some of the Union men thought Jackson was retreating.)

Just after sunset, without stopping to rest, Jackson attacked Hooker's right flank, which consisted of the Eleventh U.S. Army Corps. The surprise attack caught the Union by complete surprise—the Federals were eating supper—and the rebels destroyed the opposing force so devastatingly that the Eleventh was out of commission for the remainder of the war.

Yet, the elements of surprise and darkness, which worked so strikingly to Jackson's advantage, were also his undoing. After the initial deadly attack, Jackson's forces regrouped, reconnoitered, and Jackson went on horseback with several scouts to check the enemy's position. Confusion reigned on all sides and sporadic fighting continued. Commanders of both armies had lost track of many of their men in the darkness. Nervous soldiers, with anxious fingers on the triggers of their muskets, milled about in the surrounding wilderness unable to tell friend from foe.

For example, one Northern soldier reported wandering with five comrades, having "lost the points of the compass as completely as if there were none . . . ." The fire of nearby guns meant their eyes never completely adjusted to the darkness. The sudden flashes of gunfire "only made us all the blinder." Their confusion was confounded by "the impossibility of giving (or receiving) orders in the darkness among the tangled thickets . . . ."

This group blundered into a larger company of men. But instead of panicking, a quick-witted corporal managed to bluff the other group into surrender by calling out orders to "Captain This and Major That and Colonel Someone Else, as if he was in command of a brigade." After the surrender, the victorious group of five discovered they had captured twenty of their own company.

Jackson wasn't so lucky. As he rode back to his own lines he was mistaken for the enemy and was shot three times simultaneously. One bullet went through his palm, one through his left wrist and out through his hand, and the third splintered the large bone of his upper left arm.

Initially, it was expected that Jackson would recover from his wounds. His left arm was amputated just below the shoulder (standard treatment at the time for serious arm and leg wounds) and a bullet was removed from his right hand. But he developed a fatal case of pneumonia. Told early on a Sunday afternoon that he was about to die, he replied, "Very good; it is all right." He had always wanted to die on a Sunday. Although he spent a good part of the rest of that afternoon giving orders to invisible soldiers, his last words were: "Let us cross over the river and rest under the shade of the trees."

While on the field at Chancellorsville the Confederacy had won a smashing victory, in the farmhouse where Jackson died, the South lost one of its most powerful leaders. Many rebels would have traded the day's victory to have him back.

Battlefields were gory and ugly scenes, dotted with the bodies of soldiers and animals, and the abandoned tools of war (above).

41

While soldiers in camp were outfitted with a wide variety of clothing and equipment (right), many of the ornamental trappings were abandoned when troops were on the march against the enemy.

CLOTHING MAKES THE MILITARY MAN

When it came to clothes, despite the South's vast cotton resources, the North enjoyed a definite advantage. Although the Confederacy produced the raw materials for clothing, it had few clothing factories. As a result, its soldiers suffered from the elements far more than the Unionists. For while the North had a substantial clothing industry, the rebels generally depended on the kindness of seamsters, wives, and daughters.

For the Southerners, anything made of cloth was often in short supply.

As one rebel reported, "I had no blanket . . . I begged a copy of the *New York World* (newspaper) and lay on that, folding it up with great care every morning. I have always had a tender feeling for the *New York World* ever since."

Lack of changes of clothing intensified the Southern soldiers' problems with body lice and other parasites. As one man complained while marching through Maryland, "On this march, particularly, when the troops had no change of clean clothes for weeks, the soldiers were literally infested with (lice). Every evening, hundreds of soldiers could be seen sitting on the roads or fields with their clothes in their laps busily cracking between the two thumbnails these creeping nuisances."

For the troops, every uniform ornament had significance. This eagle (far left) adorned a cavalry sword belt. Clockwise, from top: hat cords were colored red for artillery, blue for infantry, and yellow for cavalry. Each infantry unit had its own badge (this is for the New York 7th). Cavalry shoulder scales were designed to ward off sword blows. The artillery wore little cannons. Lyre emblems were issued to company musicians.

Perhaps the worst problem of personal attire the Confederacy suffered was a lack of shoes. Even in winter many of its men had to march through the snow with raw, bleeding feet. When leather was available, some had to make do with rawhide shoes held loosely together with string. One soldier said, "They flop up and down, they stink very bad and I have to keep a bush in my hand to keep the flies off of them. This is the last of the rawhide since some of the boys got hungry last night and broiled them and ate them, so farewell rawhide shoes."

43

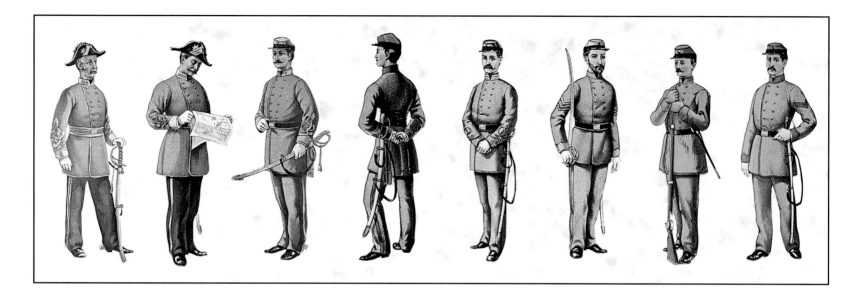

When it came to producing uniforms (above), the industrialized North enjoyed a great advantage over the South, which lacked production facilities and relied on volunteer seamstresses. Prisoners of war, however, fared badly on both sides. These prisoners (right), captured in a cavalry battle at Aldie, Virginia, could expect to face harsh conditions and receive meager rations as well as sparse clothing. Below: Confederate buttons.

The fact that many of the states in the Confederacy were obsessed with their right to rule themselves and to veto the laws of the national government exacerbated the clothing problem. At one juncture, late in the war, it was reported that while Lee's men suffered through a ragged, achingly cold winter, North Carolina warehouses were storing more than ninety-thousand pairs of shoes that were reserved for its soldiers. The governor wouldn't allow them to be worn by Virginians.

In the particularly important battle of Antietam in Maryland, which saw the bloodiest day of fighting in American history, some historians think that the lack of shoes contributed to the Confederate defeat. Maryland had something most of the other states did not—macadam roads. These roads tore up bare feet. When Confederate reinforcements marched in to shore up the Southern lines at one of the most crucial moments, they had just finished a torturous seventeen-mile march on hot, black pavement, a march severe enough to bring even the toughest soldier down. Before they faced the bullets, they were already in great pain, and their feet were bleeding. Despite their discomfort, they stood tall and still fought valiantly, but the Federals carried the day.

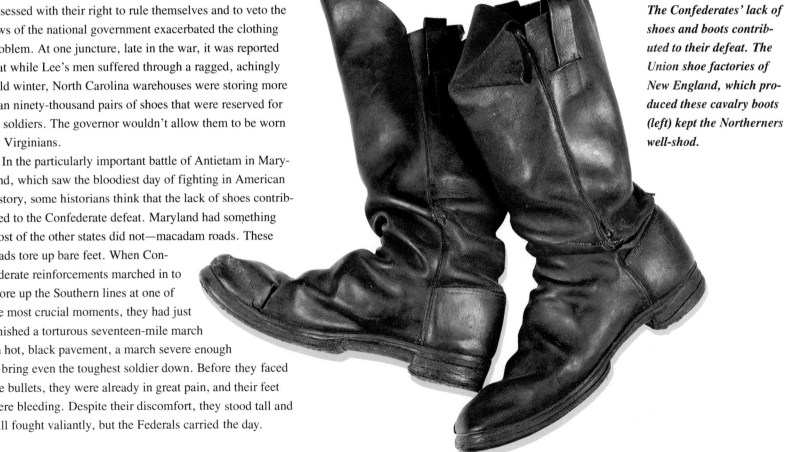

The Confederates' lack of shoes and boots contributed to their defeat. The Union shoe factories of New England, which produced these cavalry boots (left) kept the Northerners well-shod.

45

General McClellan at the Battle of Antietam (right). Although his timidity in the battle would be his undoing, Union Major General George Brinton McClellan (opposite page, left) was an expert at turning raw recruits into obedient soldiers. General McClellan's personal bodyguards, better known as the Sturges Rifles (opposite page, right), were a group of handpicked, specially trained soldiers that at one time consisted of 158 men.

GEORGE BRINTON McCLELLAN—THE HESITATING GENERAL

George Brinton McClellan, born in 1826 in Philadelphia, was an example of someone who rose to a high position in the military that he couldn't manage with competence. Blessed with early success in his military career, he took over as supreme commander of the Union forces in 1861, but that led to diastrous results because of his inadequate skills as a tactician and strategist.

McClellan's talent was in organization. If he was given an army that was disorganized and needed discipline and supplies, his "detail-oriented" mind could take care of all the loose ends that stood in the way of molding it into a fighting unit. But as a commander of an army that needed to attack and outwit its enemy, he blundered because of his innate timidity on the battlefield.

McClellan graduated second in his class at West Point in 1846. He served in the Mexican War for a few years and then became an instructor at West Point. In 1855, he was sent abroad to study the European armies and their military strategies. In 1857, unhappy with his low salary in the army, he resigned to become chief engineer of the Illinois Central Railroad.

When the Civil War started, McClellan became a major general in charge of Ohio volunteers. Then, after being commissioned into the regular army, he led forces that drove the Confederates out of West Virginia. After this success, he was given the job of organizing the troops stationed around Washington, DC, into the Army of the Potomac. Lincoln then made him the general in chief of all Federal armies.

The job of forming the Army of the Potomac was the high point of his career. He was a great success at it because of his skills in training and organizing soldiers. But once the fighting started in earnest, he looked for ways to

avoid committing his troops to combat. Time after time, he overestimated the strength of Confederate troops. Even when he obviously and substantially outnumbered the enemy, he always seemed to hesitate until the last moment, when victory was no longer possible.

McClellan procrastinated so consistently and disastrously that the press sometimes accused him of being a Southern sympathizer.

After Lincoln sacked him on November 7, 1862, General McClellan embarked on a political career that would start out with a crushing defeat but then serve him well through the remainder of his life. Convinced that Lincoln's policies were quickly leading the Union to ruin, he ran as the Democratic party candidate in the presidential election of 1864. His campaign wasn't helped by the Democratic platform that called for an immediate, negotiated end to the war. He actually advocated continuing the war to its conclusion.

McClellan soundly lost the election—212 electoral votes to twenty-one. After the war, he was the chief engineer for

More American soldiers died (22,000) on September 17, 1862, at the Battle of Antietam (inset, right), than on any other day in American military history.

the New York City Department of Docks in the early 1870s. He was also the governor of New Jersey from 1878 to 1881. He died in 1885.

ANTIETAM—BLOODIEST DAY IN AMERICAN HISTORY

In the fall of 1862, Confederate General Robert E. Lee, commander of the Army of Virginia, was marching through Maryland, attempting to invade Pennsylvania and bring the war to the Northern states. Union General McClellan and his Army of the Potomac followed him cautiously. Not knowing Lee's plan, McClellan worried that the rebels meant to march toward Washington, DC.

On September 9, in an attempt to capture Harper's Ferry, Virginia, and secure a better supply line south, Lee took a serious risk and split his army into four parts. Because of the proximity of superior Union forces, this was a very dangerous move. Lee only had about fifty-five thousand men to McClellan's ninety thousand. The split left Lee with barely more than nineteen thousand men—with McClellan nearby and possibly ready to engage. But Lee felt there was time to capture Harper's Ferry, regroup, and make a successful move north toward Harrisburg, Pennsylvania, before McClellan could stop him.

On September 13, at an abandoned rebel campsite, a Union soldier found a comprehensive copy of Lee's battle plans wrapped around three cigars. What it was doing there, no one has ever been able to explain, but it was an invaluable piece of intelligence. In detail, it revealed every part of Lee's risky maneuver. And if McClellan had used this information to strike immediately, he could have crushed Lee. The war, for all practical purposes, might have ended then and there.

Instead, McClellan waited a day, giving Lee time to get into position for battle. As a matter of fact, McClellan didn't attack in force until September 17, by which time

During the Battle of Antietam, the Antietam Bridge (left) was captured by the Northerners after a fierce firefight. Was it a mistake? The narrow bridge allowed the Confederates to inflict withering casualties on a superior enemy force. It never occurred to Union commanders to flank the Confederates by fording the shallow Antietam stream.

49

Breech-loading, repeating rifles like the Spencer (detail right and center, below) revolutionized warfare by allowing soldiers to fire much more rapidly than they could with the old muzzle loaders. The ridges on rifled bullets (below) increased the accuracy and deadliness of the projectiles by making them spin as they flew.

Technology Makes Warfare More Deadly

Although most of the rifles used in the Civil War were muskets—single-shot, older-style rifles that were loaded by pushing bullets and powder down through the barrel—many Union soldiers did use more modern weapons: repeating rifles or breechloaders with shots loaded in the compartment just above the trigger.

One revolutionary gun that the Union used to great advantage was the Spencer repeating rifle, invented by Christopher Spencer in Connecticut. It carried seven cartridges that were shoved into the chamber between shots by a lever.

While soldiers with muskets had to stop between firings and use a ramrod to shove cartridge and powder down the barrel, soldiers with the repeaters could pump out shot after shot, just hesitating a moment to work the handle that fed the firing-chamber another bullet. Only Union soldiers had access to these guns, a fact that disturbed the Confederates, especially in those battles in which they were shot down while reloading.

At a fight called the "Bermuda Hundred," Federal soldiers armed with these seven-shot repeating rifles were almost invincible. One Connecticut Yankee reported, "The Rebs made three charges on us but we stood up to the rack with our seven-shooters and piled Rebs in heaps in front of us. The Rebs hate our guns . . . call(ing) them Yanks 7 Devils. They say the G.D. Yankeys stand up their with their G.D. coffy mills, wind 'em up in the morning, run all day, shoot a thousand times."

Also available was a gun called the Henry, which could be fired sixteen times without reloading. Some Union soldiers ditched their government-issued rifles and spent all their money upgrading their firearms. It was money well-spent. As a soldier from Indiana said after paying $35 for his gun, "I think the Johnnys are getting rattled. They are afraid of our repeating rifles. They say we are not fair, that we have guns that load on Sunday and shoot all the rest of the week."

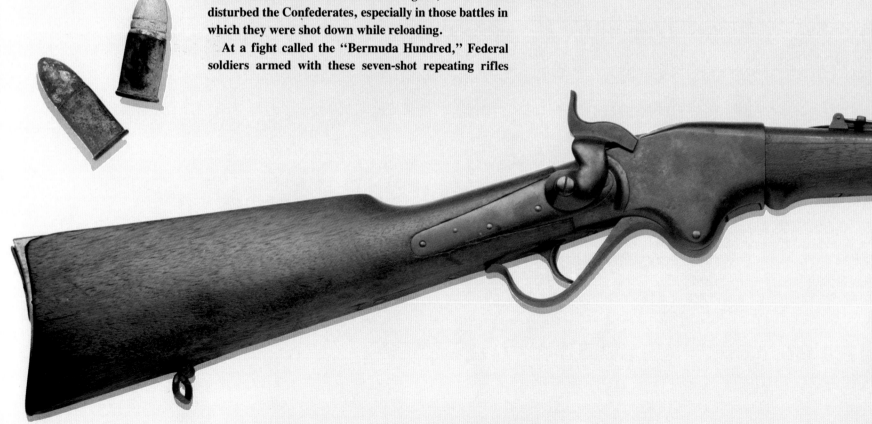

Until the Civil War, sabers had been the traditional weapon of the cavalry. But lighter, more accurate rifles secured on leather slings (above and below, left) soon became the weapon of choice.

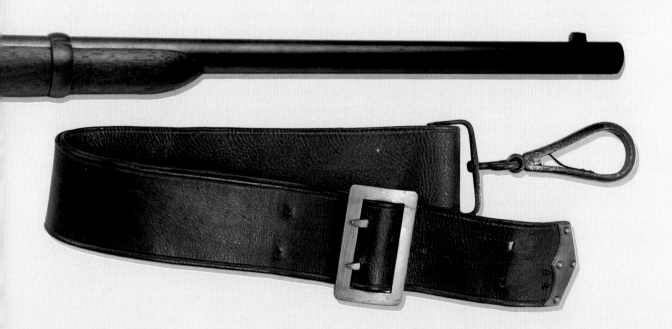

51

The hand-to-hand fighting at Antietam was deadly (right). At the end of the day, Union troops had suffered heavy casualties but had emerged victorious, crushing Lee's hopes for a successful invasion of the North.

Lee's forces were back up to more than forty thousand men, with more on the way from Harper's Ferry.

According to some historians, it is hard to describe McClellan's general plan of attack when his forces actually advanced to battle four days later. As far as anyone knows, he didn't have any plan. Instead, he allowed five of his generals with their individual units to make five different, uncoordinated assaults on the Confederates. Two other units were on the scene, but McClellan kept them on standby the entire time. They never entered the fighting.

Despite McClellan's blundering, the bloody battle spelled the end of Lee's attempt at a foray into Pennsylvania. The attacks on the Confederate flanks were scenes of appalling bloodshed. On the Confederate left, one cornfield was taken and lost by each side more than a dozen times

before noon, with a combined total of more than eight thousand casualties from both sides.

But the most astounding part of the battle took place at the center of the rebel line, in a sunken road that came to be known as "Bloody Lane." When the Confederates took cover there, it had seemed like a safe place to be. The recessed path offered some protection. But soon, Federal troops moved around the Confederate's flank and subjected the huddled, crowded rebels to withering fire: "Like shooting sheep in a pen," said one Yank.

When the Union troops advanced past the sunken road, the bodies lay so thick there was nowhere to step except on the enemy dead. One of McClellan's staff officers reported from the rear: "As the smoke and dust disappeared, I was astonished to observe our troops moving over what ap-

The Best Offense Was a Good Defense

The kinds of bullets used by both sides in the Civil War revolutionized warfare. Previously, most armies fired round bullets, which were relatively inaccurate and had a very limited range. A soldier had to be practically right on top of his opponent to be sure of getting off a worthwhile shot.

Captain Claude E. Minie, a Frenchman, used aerodynamics and some elementary physics to develop a more accurate projectile. Instead of a sphere, his bullet was a conical slug with a hollow base that, as it was fired, expanded on its way out of the barrel. Engaging the spiral rifling of the barrel as it accelerated, it gained extra spin, giving it improved range and accuracy. By expanding as it shot out of the gun, it efficiently used the power of the exploding gunpowder behind it. The older, smooth-barreled guns with round bullets let much of the firing force escape around the edges of the bullet.

The older guns were only accurate to approximately fifty yards. However, bullets of the French design could be used with confidence at almost five times that distance.

The new, long-range bullets (as well as the increasing use of repeating rifles) called for new military tactics. No longer could soldiers march across open fields and attack well-fortified positions with much hope of success unless they overwhelmingly outnumbered their opponents. Even under those conditions, the long-range armaments meant that the attacking force would suffer grievous losses.

It took generals a tragically long time to understand this change. Some never learned it at all. And years later, in Europe during World War I, the wholesale slaughter of soldiers marching across open fields against fortifications protected by machine guns would show that many military men still had not accepted this new fact of warfare.

Before the introduction of "minies" (above), rifles were only accurate to about fifty yards. The minies increased the deadliness of rifle fire to over two hundred yards. Soldiers in open fields were easy targets as these Confederate bodies along the Hagerstown Pike near Antietam (left) attest.

After Confederate soldiers at Antietam took cover in a sunken road, a flanking movement by Union troops turned the road into a deadly trap. The Northerners poured a round of devastating volleys into the Southerners whose bodies (above) quickly filled what came to be known as "Bloody Lane." At right is a harmonica lost by one of the combatants.

peared to be a long, heavy column of the enemy without paying it any attention whatever. I borrowed a glass (telescope) and discovered this to be actually a column of the enemy's dead and wounded lying along a hollow road." The dead and wounded were stacked up where they had fallen in that hellish ravine. Many of the wounded screamed and tried to crawl out from under the corpses.

In the day's fighting, Lee lost more than ten thousand men; McClellan lost twelve thousand. But the rebel total, although lower than the Union total, represented about a fourth of Lee's troops. McClellan had used forty-six thousand men and held more than twenty-four thousand in reserve for defensive purposes.

But once again, on the next day, McClellan hesitated. According to Confederate General James Longstreet, "We were so badly crushed that at the close of the day ten thou-

sand fresh troops could have come in and taken Lee's army and everything it had." McClellan had more than twice that number of well-rested men ready for action, but he wouldn't let them advance.

McClellan was satisfied with what he had done and wrote to his wife, "Our victory was complete and the disorganized rebel army has rapidly returned to Virginia, its dreams of invading Pennsylvania dissipated forever."

Other officers perceived the truth. Union officer Regis de Trobriand said, "Thus, the whole of the 18th (of September) passed away and McClellan was unable to come to the resolution to profit by this last opportunity offered him by fortune."

As for Lee, despite his defeat, he refused his subordinates' pleas for a rapid, pell-mell retreat on the morning of September 18. Instead, he stood his ground, knowing McClellan would be too cautious to make another move so soon after the bloodshed of the previous day. He also knew that his men were proud of the fact that they had never been driven from the battlefield by another army. So, although a Union attack would have brought Confederate disaster, Lee held his men in place until that evening when they fell back across the Potomac River.

Soon afterward, because of his failure to take decisive action against Lee's men, McClellan was fired from his post by Lincoln.

Soon after Antietam, Lincoln (left) met with McClellan to discuss the general's failure to chase and crush the Confederate troops of Robert E. Lee. This was the last time these two men met. Lincoln fired McClellan soon afterward.

The military genius of Robert E. Lee (opposite page, right) helped the Confederate armies prevail against superior Union forces early in the war. But his mistakes at Gettysburg combined with the industrial base the North could depend on for producing arms and ordinance, were more than he was able to overcome. Lee's house and land (right and on opposite page) were confiscated by Union forces and turned into what is now known as Arlington Cemetery.

ROBERT E. LEE—THE SOUTH'S REGAL GENERAL

It's a good thing that Robert E. Lee had a terrible temper. Otherwise he would have been too good to be true. He didn't drink, swear, smoke, or cheat on his wife (even though he spent more time on the road with his army than he did at home). As it was, the South, which was outmanned and outgunned, desperately needed a miracle general to win the Civil War. With Lee, they almost had one.

Lee came from what could be considered royal American stock. His father was a successful general in the Revolutionary War. His mother came from one of Virginia's most genteel and respected families. He married the daughter of George Washington's adopted son.

Lee graduated second in his class at West Point in 1829. After graduation, his military career involved one success

after another. In the Mexican War he was recognized for his skill, valor, and undaunted energy. As superintendent of West Point he was credited with making the academy as highly respected as Europe's best military schools. (He has the distinction of expelling the incorrigible James A. Whistler, who later became a well-known artist.)

Lee opposed forming a Confederacy. When the Southern states began to talk of secession, Lee said, "If I owned four million slaves I would cheerfully sacrifice them for the preservation of the Union." But when the Federal government offered him command of the Union army, he turned it down, saying, "Though opposed to secession and deprecating war, I can take no part in an invasion of the Southern states."

At the beginning of the war, Lee was in charge of the Confederate coastal defenses and acted as a headquarters coordinator, keeping track of how the Southern armies were positioned. On May 31, 1862, when General Joseph E. Johnston, the top Confederate general, was seriously wounded, Lee got a chance to show off his military genius.

Two of Lee's great attributes as a general were his ability to conceptualize complicated, long-range tactics, and to intuitively anticipate how his opponent would react to his moves. Tales abound about how, on little evidence, he would correctly guess when and where the Union army would strike next.

Confederate General John B. Gordon recalled how on May 7, 1864, after a battle near Fredericksburg, he discussed the Union troop movements with General Lee:

> *Reports had reached me to the effect that General Grant's army was retreating or preparing to retreat and I called General Lee's attention to these rumors. He had heard them, but they had not made the slightest impression upon (him).*
>
> *He said, "General Grant is not going to retreat. He will move his army to Spotsylvania."*

Since the Civil War predated the invention of dog tags, identification of the dead was difficult. Badges like this one, issued to the 5th Corps, 3rd Division, sometimes helped.

I asked if there was evidence of such purpose.

"Not at all," said Lee. "Not at all; but that is the next point at which the armies will meet."

Indeed, the next confrontation between the Blue and the Gray took place at Spotsylvania.

Despite his tactical acumen, Lee's situation as the military underdog eventually took its toll on the battlefield. He would have had to wage a perfect campaign to beat the North. Some might argue that he almost did. But almost wasn't good enough. He couldn't afford any mistakes. At Gettysburg, his long string of successes led him to become a little overconfident—and he made a big miscalculation. It ended his second attempt to invade the North. And it proved to be the turning point of the war.

LEE INVADES PENNSYLVANIA

After his decisive victory at the battle of Chancellorsville in the Spring of 1863, Confederate General Robert E. Lee felt the need for a change in strategy. Up until that time he had largely fought a hide-and-seek war—maneuvering his forces around the attacking Union armies, keeping his enemy off-guard with feints toward Washington and continually outflanking and usually defeating the larger forces of the opposition.

Despite the North's advantages in manpower and equipment, most of the Union generals—notably in the eastern theater of the war—moved their armies slowly and conservatively without much tactical imagination. Lee, with his amazing intuitive ability, ran circles around the enemy much to Lincoln's consternation and the South's joy.

But during the early part of the summer of 1863, Lee decided to adopt a new, bold, offensive tact, by marching north. One reason for this initiative was the desire to entice European nations into recognizing the Confederacy as an independent nation truly separate from the United States. Confederate representatives in England believed that if Lee could establish a credible offensive in the North, England and France, both of whom had taken a wait-and-see attitude toward official recognition of the secession, would lend the Confederacy money and perhaps furnish ships to break the Union blockade of Southern ports.

Lee and others also believed that taking the fight north would sap the Union's fighting spirit, since virtually all the fighting had been in the south. Southern leaders, including Jefferson Davis, the president of the Confederacy, believed that if Northerners witnessed firsthand some of the fire and blood of the war, they might lose their desire to continue the conflict.

A more pragmatic, immediate motive for heading north was the need for provisions. As usual, the Confederate soldiers were short of supplies. The army's two-plus years in Virginia had just about exhausted the available local supply of food. The rebel commissaries were having trouble keeping the army fed and clothed. It was said that when Lee requested more foodstuffs, the commissary general himself replied, "If General Lee wants rations, let him seek them in Pennsylvania." And that's what General Lee decided to do.

In Lee's view, the march into Pennsylvania would have another advantage—it would draw the Union forces away from the fortifications of Washington, where they frequently fled after being defeated by Lee's forces. If Lee could deal the Union armies a decisive blow on the far side of the Mason-Dixon line, there would be no place nearby to hide. He could beat them on the battlefield and then press his advantage and finish them off before they could hole up in Washington's strong defenses.

Unfortunately for Lee, while all these reasons for marching north seemed to make sense, the outcome of this campaign, which marked the midpoint of the war, was the beginning of the end for the South. They would find virtually no success in Pennsylvania.

Confederate Knights in Shining Gray

The skilled and daring cavalrymen who rode for the Confederacy played a large role in the early success of the rebel armies. Their cavalry superiority was based on the simple fact that the South possessed more riders than the Northern states. The warmer climate and the greater dependence on an agrarian economy made the Confederacy a natural breeding ground for horsemen. The large supply of men with horses made it possible for the Confederacy to require cavalrymen to supply their own mounts, and they saw themselves as nineteenth-century equivalents of knights on horseback, chivalrous warriors riding out to defend their homeland.

In the first years of the war, these circumstances gave the Confederates a great advantage. Little training had to be employed for men who showed up for service with their own animals. But as the conflict wore on, this temporary advantage turned into a liability. After the initial supply of mounted men was depleted by the killing machines of the war, the South possessed little provision for replacements. In contrast, once the Northern states brought their military-industrial might up to speed, they could field better-equipped, larger masses of men on horseback.

The Confederate cavalry (below, left) enjoyed an early advantage over its Union counterpart during the first stages of the Civil War. Many of the Southerners were experienced horsemen who reported for duty already equipped with spurs (below, right) and pistols and holsters (left). The Northern riders took years to catch up in skill and experience.

59

Chow lines (right) were a common sight at Union camps. So were complaints about the food. Third in line in this drawing is Walt Whitman, author of Leaves of Grass. *Below is a typical soldier's spoon.*

fall in for soup.

The Birth of Fast Food

Since most of the Union military campaigns occurred in enemy territory, on Confederate soil, the Union army was faced with the problem of transporting large quantities of food long distances. This led to the first widespread use of dried and "instant" foods that weighed less and were more easily carried by soldiers and supply wagons than conventional foodstuffs.

Extract of coffee—a kind of instant coffee—was distributed to the troops. It was not very popular among men who were used to the more full-bodied flavor of real coffee. In another innovation, the Union army also fed its troops "dessicated (sic) vegetables," dehydrated green masses that were also not as popular as the real

thing. These were "bales in a solid mass...as dry as threshed straw...contain(ing) turnip-tops, cabbage leaves, string beans...onion blades and possibly some of every other kind of vegetables....In the process of cooking it would swell up." One soldier reported that German men liked the soup that was made from these clumps, but that after one taste "native" Americans wouldn't touch "desecrated vegetables."

Some naive soldiers, unaccustomed to eating foods that had the water extracted, made the mistake of eating the dehydrated lumps without soaking them. An eyewitness account of one sorry soldier who swallowed a lump said, "We thought he was going to die...his stomach looked as if he had a bass drum in it...after quite a siege he got relief." From a culinary point of view, the war was hell.

While soldiers in camp groused about the chow churned out by company kitchens (below, center), those on sentry patrol often had to fend for themselves (left). Away from camp, canteens (below, left) and pocket knives (below, right) were invaluable tools for culinary survival.

Jeb Stuart's leadership of the Confederate cavalry was considered flawless until the battle at Brandy Station when Southerners were disappointed at his strategic errors. Some thought Stuart (right) had begun to let his sense of self-importance cloud his military judgement.

CLASH OF THE HORSEMEN AT BRANDY STATION

The beginning of Lee's trip north opened with a minor victory for the Southern cavalry that, ironically, helped the Union's cavalry gain credibility.

How could a defeat help the North? During the first two-and-a-half years of the war, the Confederate cavalry had developed a fearsome reputation. Time after time, the fast-moving cavalry scouted Northern positions—keeping Lee well-informed of his enemy's troop movements—and waged devastating hit-and-run raids on Union positions. During the initial battles, the North, with relatively few trained horsemen, was unable to field a comparable force as swift or as efficient.

In 1863, much of the South's cavalry forces were led by James Ewell Brown "Jeb" Stuart, who Lee referred to as the "eyes and ears of my army." Stuart had a nose for publicity and a flare for showmanship. Sometimes while he rode he had another man ride next to him strumming a banjo. But Stuart backed his bravado with ability. He once raided a Union army position, captured the headquarters of the unfortunate General John Pope as well as most of Pope's staff, and made off with thousands of dollars in Union greenbacks (the new, green money the North had begun printing during the war).

As Lee began his long march north, Stuart's assignment was to keep an eye on Union movements and screen Lee's flanks from attack. But at a town called Brandy Station, Virginia, the Southerners stumbled upon the Union cavalry, under its newly appointed head, Brigadier General Alfred Pleasonton.

The resulting battle happened almost by accident. The Union riders had been assigned to reconnoiter along the Confederate lines and to try to discern where the enemy was headed. But when the ten thousand Yankees crossed the Rappahannock River at five in the morning on June 9, 1863, they came across ten thousand Confederate cavalry-

The 7th New York Cavalry (above) was among the Union-mounted units that gained new respect after the Battle of Brandy Station. Each Union cavalryman was furnished a sword such as those at left. Many Confederates considered these sabers worthless.

As souvenirs, many soldiers had their pictures taken in uniform (below, right and left) or in formal dress (top). The soldiers pictured here were part of the 15th New York Cavalry. All three men survived the war. After the war, the survivors pored over these relics, which they commemorated with ribbons (bottom, center), at numerous reunions.

men. It was to be the largest cavalry engagement of the war, a striking tableau of thousands of fighting men on horseback, cavalry swords raised against each other in the morning sun.

In the midst of the ensuing battle, one of Stuart's aides, Captain William D. Farley, had a leg torn off by a cannonball. Knowing he was dying from loss of blood, Farley insisted on having his leg back. Confederate Lieutenant John T. Rhett reported:

In the second half of the war, the Union cavalry, wearers of the insignia shown at left, began to play a significant role in Union victories. Major General Alfred Pleasonton's units often sent Confederate units fleeing (below, left and right).

As the battle gained momentum, a Pennsylvania soldier, William F. Moyer, described the scene:

Just as we were about to send him away, he called me to him and, pointing to the leg that had been cut off by the ball, and which was lying nearby, he asked me to bring it to him. I did so. He took it, pressed it to his bosom as one would a child and said, smiling, "It is an old friend, gentleman, and I do not wish to part from it."

Farley died moments later.

A thousand glittering sabers flashed in the sunlight, and from a thousand . . . spirits arose a shout of defiance. . . . First came the dead, heavy crash of the meeting columns, and next the clash of saber, the rattle of pistol and carbine mingled with frenzied imprecations . . . hand to hand, face to face.

Caps and ammunition were carried in pouches (below). Scouting parties (right) were frequently the only sources of information about enemy movements.

By the end of the day Stuart, with the help of reinforcements from the infantry, beat back the Union forces. But contrary to what had been believed about its reputation for ineptitude, the Union cavalry had now established itself as a force to be reckoned with. As one Southerner, Henry McClellan, observed, the battle at Brandy Station ''made the Federal cavalry. Up to that time confessedly inferior to the Southern horsemen, they (Union cavalry) gained on this day . . . confidence in themselves and in their commanders.''

In the fighting, the North lost more than eight hundred men, the Confederates more than five hundred. One of Lee's sons was wounded, though not seriously. Most grievously injured was Stuart's reputation for invincibility. The Southern press felt that the battle had been a near disaster. One Confederate official in the bureau of war said, ''Stuart is so conceited, he got careless.''

Still, at Brandy Station, the Confederates managed to beat back the Yankees. As they proceeded north, they would not encounter this kind of good fortune in the most crucial battle of all.

The Youngest Soldiers

Although eighteen-year-olds constituted the largest single age group among the soldiers who fought in the Civil War, the conflict was remarkable for its diversity of age groups. Young boys fought alongside, and against, men who could have been their great-grandfathers. Records show that twelve-year-olds as well as seventy-three-year-olds enlisted for service on both sides.

After the war, one Confederate claimed that he was only eleven-years old when he joined the army and only fifteen when the shooting stopped. The youngest recorded Union soldier was twelve. Many of the youngest were drummer boys, but some boys carried rifles and saw heavy fighting.

In the heat of battle, these youngsters were killed or wounded as often as anybody else. But occasionally more mature soldiers would take pity on them. For example, as the Confederates marched toward Gettysburg, Captain James H. Hodam reported seeing, among a group of prisoners, a little drummer boy trying to keep up with the rest.

"Look here," I said, "you are too little to be a prisoner, so pitch the drum into that fence corner, throw off your coat, get behind those bushes, and go home as fast as you can."

The boy said, "Then you bet I am going home to mother!"

Saying this as he threw his drum one way and his coat another, he disappeared behind the fence and some bushes and I sincerely hope he reached home and mother.

The Confederate units manning the artillery at Charleston were remarkably young. The standard bearer in this 1863 portrait is all of sixteen years old.

GETTYSBURG— DISASTER FOR THE SOUTH

The medical tools used by field surgeons were crude. Usually, tools such as these (from top, saw, scalpel, forceps, probe, and pliers) were used on patients who did not have the benefit of anesthesia. Amputation was one of the most frequent medical treatments of wounds to the extremities. Devil's Den (far right) was used as a base of operations by snipers at Gettysburg.

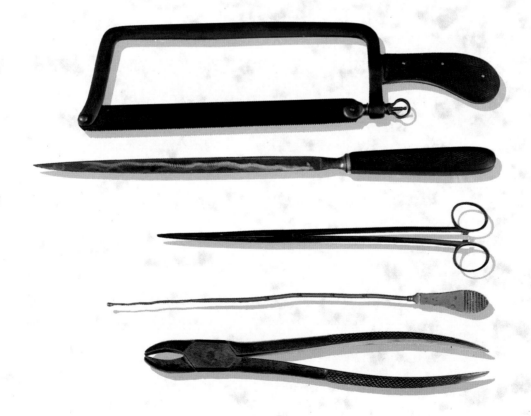

THE SHOWDOWN AT GETTYSBURG

At Gettysburg, Union commanders (below) led by General Meade stumbled upon the Confederate army, which had originally entered the Pennsylvania town in search of shoes.

A good part of Lee's motivation for marching through Pennsylvania was the need for provisions. His army was so badly supplied that they were a strange sight for the Pennsylvanians as they "conquered" the Keystone State.

Professor Michael Jacobs of Pennsylvania College described Lee's legions: "Most of the men were exceedingly dirty, some ragged, some without shoes, and some surmounted by the skeleton of what was once an entire hat, affording unmistakable evidence that they stood in great need of having their scanty wardrobe replenished. Hence the eagerness with which they inquired after shoes, hot

food, and clothing stores, and their disappointment when they were informed that goods of that description were not to be had in town."

In the late part of June, as Lee camped near Chambursburg, Pennsylvania, Stuart and the cavalry, getting wind of a huge wagon train of Union supplies at Sykesville, Maryland, captured a large shipment of food, clothing, and ammunition. Unfortunately for the Confederates, it took Stuart a long time to bring these wagons north to Lee's position. With Stuart gone and without cavalry to reconnoiter the surrounding Pennsylvania countryside, Lee's lack of information about Yankee troop movements left him guessing—incorrectly—about where his enemy was. Confederate Lieutenant William Owen complained, "(General Lee)

was evidently annoyed at the absence of Stuart . . . . The eyes and ears of the army are evidently missing and are greatly needed by the commander.''

The Union troops were much closer, and were present in much greater numbers, than Lee suspected. For, as Lee had moved north, the Union army, under the command of General Meade, had followed him every step of the way. As it was, Lee learned of the nearness of the Yankees when an advance party entered Gettysburg in search of shoes. Instead of shoes, they met gunfire and the Union cavalry. After this skirmish, both sides tried to hold their ground while sending messengers seeking reinforcements.

At the beginning of what was to be the battle of Gettysburg, on July 1, Lee's forces, closer to the town, were able to enter the field in a greater number and push the Union men southward into the town's cemetery. Cemetery Ridge, the high ground running north and south on the east side of town, became the gathering line for the Union army. Seminary Ridge (named for a Lutheran seminary), about three-quarters of a mile away from the Union lines, served as the mustering ground for the Confederates.

At the end of the first day of battle, the Confederates occupied the town but the Northerners, because of the local geography, held a more advantageous position. The lines along the ridge they defended formed a fishhook shape. At the north end, the hook was on curving high ground known as Culp's Hill. Toward the south the Federals' left flank was atop a rise called Little Round Top. Because their ridge

These mementos of the dead and wounded were abandoned at Gettysburg. Clockwise, from top: An eagle breast plate; the blade from a surgeon's saw; tooth-marked bullets that wounded soldiers were given to bite on when the pain became overwhelming; and a U.S. belt buckle.

Culp's Hill was the site of an attack on the right flank of the Union Army designed to capture Cemetery Ridge, an attack that ultimately failed.

formed a convex-shaped curve facing the enemy, the Union army's line was nearly two miles shorter than the Confederate line. Thus they were able to shift troops and maneuver reinforcements from one end of the line to the other much more quickly than the Southerners could.

That first night, camped in the cemetery, waiting for what he knew would be a colossal battle the next day, Union General Abner Doubleday reflected that the surrounding graves were "suggestive of the shortness of life and the nothingness of fame." Above his head, at the entrance to the graveyard, a sign proclaimed: "All persons found using firearms in these grounds will be prosecuted with the utmost rigor of the law." The sign would survive the hostilities. But in the ensuing battle, most of the gravestones would be blasted to pieces.

At dawn on July 2, Lee decided that the key to victory at Gettysburg was to take Cemetery Ridge away from the

Union Army. He called for two simultaneous assaults—an attack on the Union's right flank at Culp's Hill, and another against its left flank at Little Round Top.

The attack almost worked. During the morning, in the Confederates' favor, Union General Daniel Sickles abandoned his secure position on Little Round Top and advanced his troops down into an almost indefensible peach orchard in front of the hill. If it hadn't taken the Confederates until four o'clock in the afternoon to get their troops in position to attack, Sickles' move might have lost the day.

As it was, as soon as General Meade discovered that Sickles had disobeyed orders by moving forward, he sent reinforcements to the practically undefended flank. They arrived just in time. If the Union position hadn't been shaped the way it was—allowing easy access for reinforcements to be sent to either flank—the Confederates would have taken the Union left flank without much of a struggle.

Daniel Sickles, Tammany Politician Who Almost Lost Gettysburg

A unique feature of the Civil War was the presence of commanders who held their rank chiefly by virtue of their political power. Politicians who could finance and organize divisions of soldiers were given commanding rank whatever their aptitude for soldiering. One such commander was Union General Daniel Sickles, a Tammany politician from New York City. When the war started, Sickles became a colonel (and later a brigadier general) after he organized the New York Excelsior Brigade of volunteers.

Sickles was quite a colorful character. In 1852, while he was a state congressman in New York, his efforts led to New York City's purchase of Central Park. In 1857 he was elected to the House of Representatives. On February 27, 1859, while in Washington, DC, Sickles shot and killed Philip Barton Key because Key was having an affair with his wife. The murdered Key had been the United States attorney for the District of Columbia, and was also the son of Francis Scott Key, author of "The Star Spangled Banner." But Sickles got off without penalty for the murder. He pled "temporary aberration of mind"—temporary insanity. It was the first time this plea had been used.

Despite the fact that Sickles lost a leg to a cannonball at Gettysburg—he was struck down while he and his troops were overwhelmed in the peach orchard below Little Round Top—he lived a long and successful life after the war. During the postwar years, he served as a special envoy to South America. For a time, during Reconstruction, he was selected as military governor of the Carolinas. In the 1870s he was minister to Spain. In the 1890s he was again in Congress as a representative from New York City. He died in 1914 at the age of ninety-five.

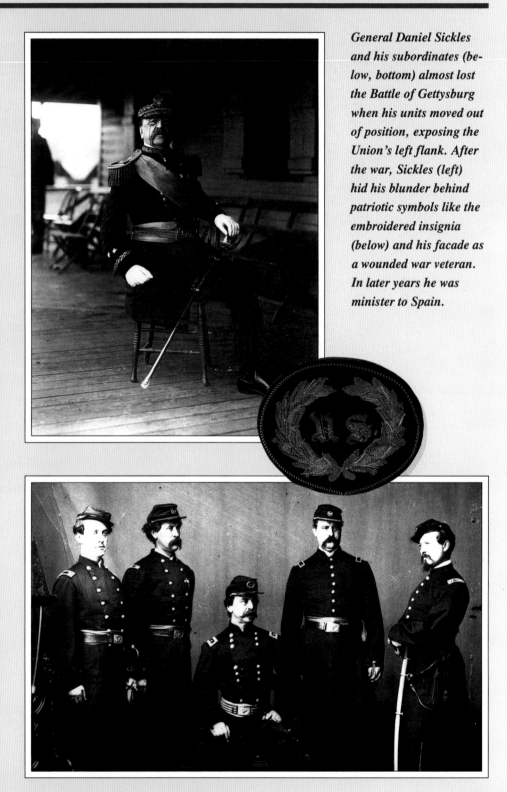

General Daniel Sickles and his subordinates (below, bottom) almost lost the Battle of Gettysburg when his units moved out of position, exposing the Union's left flank. After the war, Sickles (left) hid his blunder behind patriotic symbols like the embroidered insignia (below) and his facade as a wounded war veteran. In later years he was minister to Spain.

The scattered remnants of dead Union soldiers at Gettysburg are a grim reminder of the toll exacted by the struggle to preserve the Union.

THE BATTLE OF LITTLE ROUND TOP

As the battle was just beginning on July 2, the man General Meade sent to analyze and report on the faltering Union left flank was Brigadier General Gouverneur K. Warren, his chief engineer. When Warren reached Little Round Top, he was surprised at what he found. "There were no troops on it . . . (but) I saw that this was the key of the whole position."

From this hill, to ascertain the position of the enemy and the threat to the Union's left flank, Warren ordered a captain of a rifle battery to fire a shot into the facing woods. What Warren saw astonished him.

As the shot went whistling through the air the sound of it reached the enemy's troops and caused everyone to look in the direction of it. The motion revealed to me the glistening of gun barrels and bayonets of the enemy's line of battle . . . the line of his advance from his right to Little Round Top was unopposed . . . . The discovery was intensely thrilling to my feelings and most appalling.

Warren rode down the hill and was lucky enough to run into troops that he used to command. Although these men had been ordered elsewhere, they obeyed their former commander when he told them to defend Little Round Top. They reached their position at the summit of the hill just in time to meet a Confederate attack. One Union man said, "There was no time for tactical formation . . . . The bullets flew in among the men the moment the leading company mounted the ridge."

The Federal reinforcements had been rushed into battle so quickly they hadn't even had time to load their guns.

At the top of the hill, the bullets were thick and the casualties were heavy. Besides facing the charging Confederate army, the Union soldiers were being fired at by sharpshooters who had taken refuge in Devil's Den, an adjacent rock formation. General Stephen Weed, the ranking Union officer, was cut down almost immediately and many of the men who followed him were also killed. Union Lieutenant Porter Farley reported, "While his (Weed's) lips moving in death seemed to speak some message, gallant Hazlett stooped down to catch it, when he too was shot and fell dead upon the lifeless form of his commander." And another man who sprang up to take Hazlett's place also fell mortally wounded.

After making unsuccessful frontal assaults on Little Round Top, two Confederate Alabama regiments moved against the enemy's left flank, which just happened to be the left flank of the entire Union Army. The Confederates' losses had already been heavy. One of their commande s told how a captain "fell exclaiming, 'Oh God, that I could see my mother!' and instantly expired. . . . (Next) my dear brother . . . was pierced through by a number of bullets and fell mortally wounded. Lieutenant Cody fell mortally wounded; Captain Bethunes and several other officers were seriously wounded."

In the view of Private Theodore Gerrish, who fought with the Twentieth Maine, the Alabamian attack on the Union left flank "was a most critical moment. If that line was permitted to turn the Federal flank, Little Round Top was intenable (sic), and with this little mountain in the Confederates' possession, the whole position would be intenable." Indeed, the entire war, from the Union's point of view, might have become "intenable."

The ferocity of the fighting showed that both sides may have instinctively known that this battle would be one of the most crucial clashes of the war. If the Union line failed to hold, the entire Union effort might have come crashing down as the Southerners flanked the Union's main fighting forces on its home turf of Pennsylvania. The Alabamians charged the Mainers' position five times, and were held off five times.

Alabamian William C. Oates said, "There never were harder fighters than the Twentieth Maine men and their gallant colonel (Joshua L. Chamberlain) . . . . My dead and wounded were then nearly as great in number as those still on duty. They literally covered the ground. The blood stood

The use of cannons like the one pictured here (above, left) were of vital importance at Gettysburg. Bayonets like the one at left were rarely used by Civil War soldiers. It was considered more effective to wield the rifle as a club. The ring (far left) is all that's left of a soldier's pocket watch.

Little Round Top at Gettysburg (right) was almost lost to a Confederate advance when General Sickles abandoned it. Reinforcements led by General Warren pushed the Southerners back.

in puddles in some places on the rocks; the ground was soaked with blood.''

Finally, out of desperation or in a moment of fortuitous inspiration, Colonel Chamberlain gave his Maine men the order to ''Fix bayonets!'' and then ''Charge bayonets!'' Chamberlain's suddenly conceived plan from the top of the hill was to ''Hold fast by our right and swinging forward to our left, (make) an extended right wheel, before which the enemy's second line broke and fell back.'' His line of men swung around, like a ''gate upon a post,'' flanked the Alabamians and shocked them into surrender and flight. The Union left flank, and the Union cause, had held.

During that day, July 2, 1863, at other areas of the battle, the advantage had wavered back and forth between the two opposing armies. After advancing a few yards, the Northerners had fallen back to their lines along the ridge. The Confederates had advanced slightly on the Union right flank and held positions on Culp's Hill. By nightfall, it seemed clear that the next day's battle would decide who would be victorious.

On July 3, Lee decided that a frontal assault on the Union's center combined with an attack led by Jeb Stuart against Union troops occupying the rear was the Confederacy's best chance to defeat the Yankees. This strategy would turn out to be a huge mistake. The superior weaponry available to defenders of the Union's entrenched positions made such an attack tantamount to suicide.

Some of Lee's commanders had already learned this lesson of the new war technology. From firsthand experience, they knew that the range and accuracy of rifled musket bullets and 1860s artillery had rendered open-field charges on well-fortified troops—such as the Union men along Cemetery Ridge—virtually ineffective.

Lee's second-in-command, General James Longstreet, argued against the assault. ''General Lee,'' he said, ''there never was a body of fifteen thousand men who could make that attack successfully.'' But Lee held firm in his decision.

Because of the enormity of the task, there were signs of indecision on the Confederate side. On July 3, when the Confederate Chief of Artillery E. Porter Alexander was

This view from Little Round Top near the Battle of Gettysburg (inset) looks northward across the field where Pickett's ill-fated charge was cut to pieces by Union fire.

Confederate General James Longstreet (right) argued against sending General Pickett across an open field to attack dug-in Union troops at Gettysburg, but Lee, anxious for a decisive Confederate victory, overruled his objections.

given Longstreet's order to soften up the Union position with a morning bombardment before the charge, he was told that if his shells didn't seem to demoralize the Yankees, he—Alexander, himself—could call off the attack.

Alexander was shocked to have this kind of responsibility thrown upon him. The artillery chief, who was low on ammunition, said he thought the attack was a bad idea, and if they wanted to call it off, they should do so immediately before he used up what little ammo he and the entire Confederate army had left. Despite the objections, Longstreet told Alexander to start firing and report what effect the shelling had on the Northerners.

The Confederate attack was to be led by General George Pickett, whose men had recently arrived on the scene. Pickett's divisions—consisting of fifteen thousand men—had seen little action recently and were by far the most rested in the army.

After half an hour of exchanging artillery fire with the Federal batteries, Alexander saw the Union men withdraw their guns. He didn't know what that meant. The Confederates had often interrupted their gunning to save powder and shells, but he had never seen the Union Army do so. By courier, he told Pickett to charge at that moment, since the chance might not come again. (It turned out that Union artillery was also saving on ammunition, although they weren't as low on shells as the Confederates were.)

Just before Pickett led his ill-fated charge, he asked General Longstreet for last-minute instructions. Longstreet couldn't speak—he was crying. Believing he was likely to die in the attack, Pickett wrote a good-bye note to his fiancée and handed it to Longstreet.

Perhaps Lee ordered the charge because he truly believed his troops, no matter what the circumstances, were unbeatable. Certainly, as Pickett's men advanced, one Union defender observed, "They came on in magnificent order, with the step of men who believed themselves invincible."

But the withering Union fire tore most of the Confederate divisions to pieces. Sporadically, Confederate forces would breach the Federals' lines, but quick reinforcements almost immediately drove the Southerners off.

When the charge led by General George E. Pickett (left) was repulsed at Gettysburg, Lee's advance into Pennsylvania had ended in failure. Confederate forces would never invade the North again in any significant numbers. This six-pound Confederate cannonball (below) was found at Gettysburg.

In one dramatic moment, Confederate General Lewis A. Armistead captured a Union position. To urge his men on, he put his hat atop his sword and waved it wildly. He was quickly shot down. As the Confederate general lay dying, an old friend of his—Union General Winfield Scott Hancock, who fought at that Union position—was shot down from his horse and fell next to him, although he was not seriously wounded. Two years earlier, the two men had served together at a small army town in California—Los Angeles—before Armistead had quit the U.S. Army for the Confederacy. Before he died, Armistead handed his personal effects to his good friend, Hancock, to give to his family.

Gettysburg was a great Union victory, but, by not pursuing Lee's fleeing troops, who had their backs up against the Potomac River, Union General Meade let an even greater victory slip from his grasp. Here (right), Meade's troops cross the Potomac more than two weeks after the battle, long after Lee's forces escaped to safety.
The day that Lincoln gave his Gettysburg Address, the small Pennsylvania town (opposite page) was mobbed with soldiers, dignitaries, and government officials.

The entire Confederate attack at Gettysburg was the disaster that Longstreet had feared. One newsman reported, "The (rebel) lines have disappeared like a straw in a candle's flame. The ground is thick with the dead, and the wounded are like the withered leaves of autumn. Thousands of rebels throw down their arms and give themselves up as prisoners."

At the same time as Pickett's forces were being blasted off the field, Jeb Stuart's attempt to attack the Union rear flanks was also stopped. The Union cavalry under the leadership of General George Custer beat back Stuart's men with daredevil charges. After several clashes, using the kind of fearless, and perhaps foolhardy, tactics that would later ensure the massacre of Custer and his men at Little Big Horn, all threats to the Federals from Confederate horsemen came to a halt.

When the day ended in ignominious defeat, Lee admitted, "It was all my fault." He took his army back toward Virginia. Because of recent rains, he and his tattered army were forced to wait on the northern shore of the Potomac until the river went down.

Many observers, including Abraham Lincoln, felt that if Meade had attacked Lee as he fell back, the Army of Virginia could have been wiped out. Even the Union men knew the Confederates were low on ordinance. Several wounded Federals pointed out that they had been shot with nails instead of bullets.

But Meade refused to press his advantage. He was happy to celebrate his victory. He crowed that his purpose had been "to drive from our soil every vestige of the presence of the invader."

Lincoln replied to Meade, "My God, is that all?" Lincoln likened Meade's timid pursuit of Lee to "an old woman trying to shoo her geese across a creek."

On July 13, Lee crossed back into Virginia. His army never returned to Pennsylvania. He offered to resign his post, but Jefferson Davis, president of the Confederacy, insisted he stay on as general of the Confederate army.

THE NORTH'S VICTORIOUS CAMPAIGN

Because most of the fighting took place on Southern soil, Southerners suffered much more from the war than Northern citizens. Here (right) Federal gun batteries face Yorktown, Virginia, as Union troops laid siege to the town. Many of the dead were buried near where they fell, as in this military cemetery (far right) at Vicksburg.

Despite his reputation for drinking, Ulysses S. Grant eventually gained Lincoln's confidence and was awarded overall command of the Union armies. His nickname, "Unconditional Surrender" Grant, came about after he accepted the unconditional surrender of Fort Donelson, Tennessee.

ULYSSES S. GRANT— UNRELIABLE DRUNK BECOMES WAR HERO

On superficial inspection, Ulysses S. Grant was as ordinary as Robert E. Lee was regal. While Lee was known for his distinguished bearing, good manners, and striking personal presentation, Grant was described as having "nothing marked in his appearance. He had no gait, no station, no manner, rough, light-brown whiskers, a blue eye and rather a scrubby look withal."

If it could be said that the aristocratic Lee stood for the old order that was about to be swept away in a tidal wave of bloody warfare, then Grant symbolized the more practical, less dashing but efficient spirit of the modern military-industrial war machine. In his fighting style, Grant showed that persistence and superior technology were more important than intangible factors like valor and chivalry. It might be better to have both technology and valor, but the side that could launch the most bullets and shells would ultimately win. Grant turned out to be the leader uniquely suited to pressing the North's firepower advantage.

Born Hiram Ulysses Grant, he became "Ulysses S." from a clerical error made when he enrolled at West Point. And while Lee came from the equivalent of American royalty—a family that saw distinguished service in the Revolution and owned plantations—Grant sprung from a more pragmatic family, successful in commerce and politics.

As a boy, Grant was known for being able to break wild horses. In the classroom the only subject that he excelled in was mathematics. He was tone deaf and hated music. He said that he knew two songs: "One was Yankee Doodle and the other wasn't." He had no sense of rhythm either and couldn't keep in step when marching with others.

Grant's father was in the tanning business. After he had been elected the mayor of Georgetown, Maryland, he got his son into West Point. It was a good thing the older Grant wasn't set on his son going into the tanning business, since the young boy disliked it.

When Grant first reported to West Point he was seventeen years old, barely five feet tall and weighed less than 120 pounds—hardly the image of the man who would later save the Union. Fellow cadets called him "Country Sam," because he looked and moved like a hick from the sticks. But he gained respect for his horsemanship. It was said that he could tame wild horses as a giant would handle a child.

After graduating from West Point, he hoped to become a math professor at the academy. When no vacancies opened up, he was sent into the Mexican War—a conflict he thought was morally wrong and an ill-conceived American attempt to annex Mexican territory. Nonetheless, he served there with distinction, and also met most of the officers who would later command the Confederate armies. During the Mexican War, General James Longstreet, who was to become Lee's second in command, said that in battle Grant was "always cool, swift and unhurried . . . as unconcerned as if it were a hailstorm instead of a storm of bullets."

But after the Mexican War, he was assigned to duty on the West Coast. There, bored and unable to get along with his superiors, he began the heavy drinking that would tarnish his reputation for the rest of his life. Eventually, he

Although photographers captured much of the war's effects and participants on film, the long time exposure they needed for their pictures militated against action shots. Illustrations like this Currier and Ives' drawing of the Battle of Chattanooga (below) were used to convey the flavor of battle.

quit the service, ostensibly to become a farmer, but he wasn't very successful at it. He failed at selling firewood, then aborted an attempt to sell real estate. Finally, his father gave him a job keeping the ledgers at his retail store in Galena, Illinois.

When the Civil War started, Grant helped train Illinois volunteers. He was soon appointed a colonel. That was followed by a leadership role in Tennessee. His tactical ability and his early successes along this western front began to bring him widely acclaimed approval. When Confederate Brigadier General Simon B. Buckner surrendered Fort Donelson to Grant in Tennessee, he tried to negotiate terms. Grant replied, "No terms except an unconditional and immediate surrender can be accepted. I propose to move immediately upon your works." Afterwards, the initials "U.S." in Grant's name became known as "Unconditional Surrender."

Because of the complicated politics of the U.S. War Department, and the bureaucratic infighting that went on among the Union commanders, it wasn't until after Grant took Vicksburg, Mississippi, and then secured all of Tennessee for the Federals, that Lincoln made him the chief commander of all the Union forces. Grant coordinated all Union movements against the Confederacy in steady, constant aggressive action, something that the previous U.S. commanders had never been able to accomplish. Although some argue that he lacked the brilliant military creativity of Lee, Grant not only saw what needed to be done for the North to win the war, but he had the organizational ability to see that his plans were carried out effectively.

THE CONFEDERACY LOSES VICKSBURG AND THE MISSISSIPPI RIVER

The defeat at Gettysburg was only half of the disaster the Confederacy suffered through during the first week of July 1863. On the very same day as their defeat there at Gettys-

It was rumored that when Grant hit the bottle, members of his staff (shown here with their commander) had to hide the liquor. Regardless of his shortcomings, he still enjoyed more success than any other Union general.

Maintaining long supply lines of wagon trains (left) was a constant strategic headache for both armies. Grant's attacks on Vicksburg succeeded in part because he abandoned his own supply lines, a move that confused the Confederates. As they marched, many Confederates abandoned their bayonets (below), which they hardly ever used.

burg, on July 3, Union General Ulysses S. Grant captured the city of Vicksburg, Mississippi, a key position controlling the lower Mississippi River.

Grant, the head of the Union's Army of Tennessee, had been trying to take this heavily fortified town since the end of 1862. It was the last bastion of Confederate power on the Mississippi. Virtually every other important Mississippi port had by that time been occupied by the Federals.

Both Grant and Lincoln knew that with the capture of Vicksburg, the entire river could be controlled by Union forces. Once the river was under blockade, the eastern half of the Confederacy would be deprived of foodstuffs it needed from the western half. In addition, under Union control the river could then be used to transport troops along the length of the Confederacy. But so long as Vicksburg remained in Confederate hands, Federal efforts to conquer the west would be hampered.

For several reasons, the capture of Vicksburg was a difficult tactical objective for the Union forces. It sat on steep bluffs with a commanding view of the eastern bank of the Mississippi and surrounding territory, making it impossible to attack from the river. The bluffs were so high, gunboats couldn't aim high enough from the water to threaten the city's defenders. The other side of the city, away from the river, was largely protected by swamp.

Four times, Grant tried to take Vicksburg by conventional military methods, and failed four times. First he tried a pincer action from the northeast and northwest. But rebel cavalry, under the command of Nathan Bedford Forrest, destroyed communications between the two pincers and cut off Grant's supply lines.

The next attempt occurred when Grant tried to cut a channel through a peninsula across the river from Vicksburg and approach the city from downstream. Two months of channel digging ended in failure.

For his third try, Grant attempted to float gunboats across the swampy, steamy delta north of Vicksburg. Snakes, vegetation, and rebel sharpshooters turned the boats back. After that initial abandoned attempt, they tried again through another delta for the fourth unsuccessful attempt at Vicksburg.

Grant was under heavy political pressure to succeed. Critics in government and in the press argued that he was running the campaign all wrong. He complained that "Because I would not divulge my ultimate plans . . . they pronounced me idle, incompetent, and unfit to command men . . . and clamored for my removal."

One reporter accused Grant of being a "drunken imbecile." But Lincoln stood by him, saying, "If I knew what brand of whiskey he drinks, I would send a barrel of it to all my other generals." At least Grant carried the fight to the enemy. Lincoln was tired of timid generals who were afraid to attack.

Confederate General J. C. Pemberton (above, right) was forced to surrender Vicksburg (right) to Grant when his troops ran out of food and threatened mutiny.

Although big Confederate guns like the one nicknamed "Whistling Dick" (left) prevented an attack on Vicksburg from the Mississippi River when the Union siege cut off supplies from the town, the heavy artillery couldn't save the Southern forces from surrender.

Faced with few alternatives, Grant tried the unconventional. Abandoning his own supply lines, he moved his army downriver of Vicksburg, crossed the Mississippi and moved inland. His men would have to live off the land, which they did, stripping farmers and the local citizenry of everything the Union forces could use to further their efforts. When a Mississippi farmer on a mule complained to one of the generals that marauding soldiers had taken everything of value from his land, the unsympathetic general threatened to confiscate the mule.

To distract the Confederates while Grant moved downriver, Union General William Tecumseh Sherman made a diversionary attack against the rebels north of Vicksburg. The distraction worked. Confederate General John Pember-

ton, the rather dull-witted old soldier who commanded the South's Vicksburg troops, was thrown into confusion by Grant's unorthodox tactics. Pemberton sent troops north to ward off Sherman's fake assault. Then Pemberton sent other rebels to cut off Grant's line of supply—even though Grant essentially had no supply line to cut off. Still other Confederates who were needed to defend Vicksburg were dispatched southward to fight Union cavalry who were under the command of Benjamin H. Grierson.

Grant crossed the Mississippi downstream of Vicksburg on April 30, 1863. By the middle of May he had fought Pemberton in five battles and won every one. After the last decisive Union victory, Grant drove the rebels back into the city, which was protected by its bluffs and extensive

The Union shelling of Vicksburg (right) marked one of the first times soldiers fired artillery shells (below) at civilian targets.

fortifications, still securely in Confederate control. Even though Pemberton's troops had lost all semblance of morale, Grant still lost thousands of men trying to assault the city directly.

At this point, by the end of May, Grant decided to sit and starve the rebels out. They had no hope of being reinforced or resupplied. The Confederate forces inside the city numbered about twenty thousand men. Grant had gathered a siege force of more than seventy thousand men that cut off all escape routes from the city.

During the siege, the world witnessed a new wrinkle in modern warfare. Union forces not only fired on the defending troops, but they also lobbed artillery shells into the heart of the city, striking directly into the heart of the civilian population. This tactic was to become a commonplace practice in future wars.

One Vicksburg citizen wrote, "Hardly any part of the city was outside the range of the enemy's artillery . . . . Mortars were put in position and trained directly on the homes of the people." To protect themselves, the populace dug underground bunkers that were impervious to the bombardment. As food supplies dwindled, cats and dogs either starved to death or were eaten by the townspeople. A woman found that "rats are hanging dressed in the market for sale with mule meat. There is nothing else."

In constant peril and slowly starving, the residents of Vicksburg underwent such mental stress as would wear down their endurance. "Powerless to resist the tide of events," said one civilian, "(our) only refuge is in the indulgence of a desperate hope, whose alternative is despair and madness."

Finally, at the end of June, Pemberton's troops, starving and demoralized, handed their commander an ultimatum: "If you can't feed us, you had better surrender us, horrible as the idea is." Otherwise, the men threatened to desert.

Pemberton decided to surrender on the Fourth of July. "I know we can get better terms from them on (that day) than on any other date of the year."

After surrendering, the Vicksburg inhabitants awaited the approach of the Union conquerors with trepidation. But

the entrance of the Federals actually meant relief from the unbearable conditions under which they had been living. The surrender halted the shelling of the city. The Northerners brought food and provisions.

In her observation of Grant's victorious Union army, a Southern belle witnessed a turning point in the war and looked upon the changing face of modern warfare: "Civilization, discipline, and order seemed to enter (the city) with the measured tramp of those marching columns; and the heart turns with throbs of added pity to the worn men in gray (the Confederates) who were being blindly dashed against this embodiment of modern power." For the Confederates, their valor and fighting spirit without food and ammunition was certainly no match for the Union's modern war machine.

Under the terms of the ceasefire, "Unconditional Surrender" Grant actually let conditions be set allowing most of the rebels to return home. Unknowingly, though, Pemberton had set up the Confederacy for a double blow—both Vicksburg and Gettysburg were lost in the same week. Southern spirits were crushed by the double defeat. This news effectively ended any hope that European nations would recognize the Confederacy and come to its aid.

Following Vicksburg, General Grant, the Union commander who won the most battles, was named by Lincoln to head all the Federal armies. Previously, Lincoln had promoted and dismissed his other top generals an average of once every three and a half months. But Grant was to be his last choice, since he would lead the Union forces until the bitter end of the war.

When Union troops entered Vicksburg on July 4, 1863, Grant's victory coincided with Meade's success at Gettysburg. This event was a double blow for the Confederacy.

The War Boosts Prostitution

A wartime industry that benefited greatly from the Civil War was prostitution. Thousands of men on both sides, away from home for the first time, partook of the kind of pleasure from ladies of leisure that was unavailable in their small native burgs.

During the war years, it is said, Washington, DC, with its thousands of troops, became the sex capital of the country. More than four hundred houses of prostitution were counted by one Washington newspaper. The ranks of the prostitutes were filled by more than six thousand women.

Long queues of sheepish soldiers often stood outside these establishments, waiting to turn over their money for a few minutes of commercial sex. At the time, there were no laws against prostitution and it was practiced openly. Neither the Confederate nor the Union army ever took any measures against it.

The proprietress of one notorious Washington house hung a sign over its entrance that read "Hooker's Headquarters," named after "Fighting" Joe Hooker, one of the Union's more flamboyant generals. Thanks to the fame of this house of ill-repute, prostitutes have been known as "hookers" ever since.

Prostitution was legal during the Civil War. Legend has it that prostitutes acquired the nickname of "hookers" because of the regular patronage of the troops of Union General Joseph Hooker (right).

THE SOUTH ACCEPTS DEFEAT

The McLean house (opposite page), where the Civil War officially ended, as it looks today. Many of the trinkets carried by Civil War soldiers are now collector's items. The book at right was issued by the U.S. Sanitary Commission; it contains hints and aids for the busy soldier as well as devotional messages. The cards (far right), dice, and pipe bowls provided nocturnal, around-the-campfire solace for troops on the move.

Despite its agrarian economy, the South faced severe food rationing (right) because federal troops destroyed its farms. Much of the South's land was used for growing non-food crops like cotton and tobacco.

FOOD SHORTAGES WEAKEN THE CONFEDERACY

Since most of the Civil War was fought in the South, its citizens suffered the most from the havoc caused by the constant battles. Unfortunately, as a society, the South was ill-prepared to deal with the difficulties of what turned into a nasty, long war. Its economic health depended on trade with others. Largely an agrarian society, the pre-war Confederacy sold its major goods—primary commodities such as tobacco and cotton—to the Northern states or to European nations to make money and keep its economy healthy.

So when the Civil War disrupted interstate and international commerce, the Confederacy's financial woes multiplied rapidly. To raise much of the cash needed to finance the war, the Confederacy simply printed more and more paper currency—called "fiat" money—without much to

back it up. When the central Confederate government tried to collect taxes from states, many of them simply passed along the valueless paper money.

In February 1862, when the Confederate Congress asked President Jefferson Davis what he needed to win the war, he said he wanted 300,000 more men, 750,000 more rifles, five thousand cannons, five thousand tons of powder, and sixty more ships. Unfortunately, there was no possible way to supply any of this.

For the average Confederate citizen, particularly for those residents in cities, the unstable financial situation gave rise to severe inflation. By the beginning of 1862 the price of coffee in Richmond had doubled since the start of the war. Butter had gone from twenty-five cents a pound to forty cents. Whiskey had more than doubled in price to $1.50 a gallon.

It would have seemed that the Confederacy, with its many farms and plantations, should at least have been able to feed itself adequately during the war, but that wasn't the case. For one thing, much of the South's agricultural capacity was devoted to cash crops such as tobacco and cotton, which couldn't be eaten.

And when the Union army cut railroads and captured roads, farmers who did grow food had no way to get their produce into the urban areas. Then when the Union army marched through southern territories, living off the land and confiscating farmers' crops, that action also took food out of the mouths of the local citizenry.

Added to these woes was the fact that many of the best farmers were in the army. Women, children, and slaves tried to keep the farms going, but there was too much work to be done. As the war rolled on, the food situation went from bad to worse.

By 1863, in Richmond, the Confederate capital, the lack of food, and the high prices of what was available almost

led to a full-scale rebellion. The food situation that spring was exacerbated by the fact that the citizens had to share what little they had with the nearby Confederate troops. A local newspaper estimated that the average family food bill had, by this time, climbed to more than ten times what it was before the war.

On April 2, 1863, a group of disgruntled Richmond women gathered at a Lutheran Church and then took to the streets. By the time they reached the mansion of Virginia governor John Letcher, hundreds of others had joined them. They complained to Letcher about the lack of food. He claimed he could not help them.

The crowd moved on and by the time it entered downtown, disgruntlement had led to riot. The demonstrators soon turned to looting the stores and shops. Most of the people only wanted food, but many took whatever they could carry. Finally, Jefferson Davis brought in troops to stop the disturbance.

This "bread riot" in Richmond was not an isolated incident. Similar violence broke out in the spring of 1863 in Atlanta and Macon, Georgia, as well as in towns in North Carolina and in Mobile, Alabama.

The shortage of flour in the Confederacy sparked bread riots in Richmond (below, left), the Confederate capital. Confederate money (below, right) quickly lost its value as inflation ran riot in Dixie.

Jefferson Davis, president of the Confederacy, was blamed by many Southerners when the war started to go badly. Afterward, his harsh imprisonment by the federal government restored his popularity south of the Mason-Dixon line.

JEFFERSON DAVIS— RELUCTANT CONFEDERATE PRESIDENT

Born in a four-room log cabin in Kentucky, Jefferson Davis never wanted to be president of the Confederacy. He would have preferred a commission in its army. His stiff personality and unyielding character hindered his efforts as a politician. His psyche was always better suited to commanding men in uniform. In civilian life, executive orders were open to discussion, a practice Davis had a hard time abiding. As a result of Davis's difficulty in relating to people who disagreed with him, by the end of the war even his own vice president, Alexander Stephens, wasn't on speaking terms with him.

Like so many others who played prominent roles in the Civil War, Davis had been to West Point. There, he was close friends with Albert S. Johnston and Leonidas Polk, future Confederate generals. He also met Robert E. Lee—who was to become the South's hero—and Joseph E. Johnston who was also to lead Confederate troops.

After he was wounded during the war with Mexico, Davis' need for crutches enhanced his image as a military hero and helped get him elected to the Senate from Mississippi. In 1852, after losing a race for the Mississippi governorship, he went back to farming and gardening until President Franklin Pierce made him secretary of war. He was very effective as head of the military. He introduced the use of the deadly accurate "Minie" bullet and created the military medical service. His one failure was in trying to get the army to use camels for transportation. Everyone else preferred railroads.

After leaving Pierce's cabinet in 1857, he was reelected to the Senate where he became an outspoken proponent of the Southern view on slavery and states' rights. He was opposed to secession, but when the Confederacy was formed, his allegiance was to his state—Mississippi—not to the national government.

Because of the difficulties he had with people who disagreed with him or questioned his authority, Davis gained a reputation as an incompetent, rigid leader who refused to acknowledge the overwhelming odds stacked against the South. He should have recognized that the North's twenty-two million people versus the South's nine million (including slaves), and the Union's formidable industrial strength made the Confederate struggle a risky gamble at best. But he stubbornly believed that the South would be victorious.

When things started to go wrong for the South, few wanted to blame the beloved Robert E. Lee. Davis, with his cold-fish personality, made a better target. When the army started losing, the Confederates blamed Davis for hampering Lee's efforts and his popularity plummeted.

At the end of the war, the Federals arrested Davis, putting him in irons. The harsh conditions of his imprisonment reincarnated him as a hero to Southerners. Except for Lee, Davis was forever after the symbol of the South's resistance to the "damned Yankees."

After he was released from prison, Davis spent the last quarter century of his life defending the Confederate states' right to secede. Yet, just before he died at the age of eighty-one, he could see a bright future for the country he had worked to tear apart. In a letter, he described "a future full of golden promise, a future of expanding national glory before which all the world shall stand amazed."

During the war, Northerners swore they would hang Jefferson Davis from a tree if they ever caught him. Cards embellished with "Jefferson Davis Neckties" (below) enjoyed great popularity at the time.

The Jeff. Davis' "Neck-tie."
S. C. Upham, 310 Chestnut St.

After the war ended, bodies continued to be buried for years. Cold Harbor, where thousands were killed, was only one location where bodies were gathered for proper burial after the shooting stopped.

BURN AND CONQUER THE SOUTH

Soon after Grant became the Union's top general, he instituted an overall Federal battle plan that included laying waste to the Confederacy's economic infrastructure. Starting in the spring of 1864, Grant ordered his armies to take the offensive on three fronts: the Army of the Potomac would move directly south to try and flank Lee's forces; General Benjamin Butler's men would threaten Richmond; and General Sherman along with others in the west would move through Tennessee and then slash and burn their way to Atlanta.

Grant's march southward with the Army of the Potomac was a bloody series of completely unsuccessful flanking moves that Lee constantly thwarted at great expense to both sides. In one month, during this heavy war of attrition, Grant lost a total of fifty-five thousand men—the equivalent of all of Lee's forces. While Grant could certainly afford these kinds of losses, Lee, who lost fewer soldiers, was left in worse shape because of his already more limited resources.

But in the Northern press, Grant was criticized for inflicting such heavy casualties. Newspapers started referring to him as a "butcher." It didn't help that a modern invention, the camera, was graphically picturing the carnage caused by the battles. Although the photographs couldn't be reproduced in newspapers and magazines, they were displayed in galleries in the major Northern cities. Drawings and lithographs made from the photos appeared in publications like *Harper's* magazine as well as in the big city newspapers.

MATHEW BRADY BRINGS PHOTOGRAPHY TO THE BATTLEFIELD

It is ironic that much of the life of Mathew Brady, a pioneer in the use of photography to record historical events, should be cloaked in ambiguity. His exact date of birth is unknown. Where he was born is not certain. Even the date of his death on his tombstone—1895—is wrong. He died in 1896. No one can even be sure exactly which of the pictures bearing Brady's name were actually taken by him. As the head of his own photographic studio, with many assistants and staff photographers, Brady did not personally take all the pictures that are credited to him. He suffered from numerous eye ailments that curtailed his picture taking.

When the Civil War began, the practice of photography was still in its infancy. Barely two decades before, in 1839, Louis Jacquest Mande Daguerre, a Frenchman, had invented the "daguerreotype," an image formed on copper plates by the chemical interaction of iodine and silver. Later, technical innovations on this process allowed photographers to produce images on paper.

Born in 1823 or 1824 in Ireland or upstate New York, Mathew Brady set up his own photography studio in 1844 in New York City on Broadway. While most other photographers focused their energies on making a living from

Photo taken July 22 1861

BRADY The Photographer returned from Bull Run

Mathew Brady largely abandoned his successful New York photography studio to go south and document the Civil War. While the battle brought him fame as a war photographer, it almost ruined him financially. At the time, few were interested in purchasing pictorial reminders of the painful conflict.

taking people's portraits, "Brady of Broadway" decided to take photographs of all distinguished Americans in a historical record that he planned to publish in one big book.

In this gallery of "the men and mothers of America," he included the dying Andrew Jackson, who had been the seventh president of the United States. He took pictures of writers, including Edgar Allen Poe and Washington Irving. In 1847, he opened a Washington gallery and photographed President Polk and his cabinet. Later, in 1849, his pictures of President Zachary Taylor and his cabinet would be the first published pictures of a chief executive and his staff.

In February 1860, when Abraham Lincoln came to New York City to give his speech at Cooper Union, one of Lin-

Taking and developing photographs in the field was a time-consuming, equipment-intensive process. These wagons, the property of photographer Sam A. Cooley, served as portable darkrooms as the photographers followed the soldiers.

Action scenes had to be posed, for the cameras of the day were too slow to capture movement. These artillerymen (left) posed at Fredericksburg for their portrait by Andrew J. Russell. The photographers also made money doing portraits of the soldiers that they could send home (below).

coln's first stops was at Brady's Broadway studio to have his portrait taken. Currier and Ives later made this picture into a lithograph that was widely distributed. Lincoln later said, "Brady and the Cooper Institute made me president."

When the war started, Brady had a great advantage over other photographers who were trying to get permission to accompany the armies into the field. As a longtime photographer of rich, famous, and politically connected people, Brady already knew most of the men who were becoming Union generals. His personal connections made it easy for him to find out where the action was and to get there with his camera, or send one of his staff.

As the war progressed, photographers became a fixture on the battlefield. In those days, taking pictures was a cumbersome business. The large glass photographic plates had to be exposed in the camera for at least thirty seconds or more; therefore, most of the pictures taken in the field were posed scenes. Those that showed action were most often blurred. Also, photographers had to bring to the bat-

The Civil War caught the United States' medical community unprepared for the vast number of wounds it was called upon to treat. This tool (above) was used to drill into the skull. In the field, doctors frequently had to operate under the most primitive conditions, often out of doors (right).

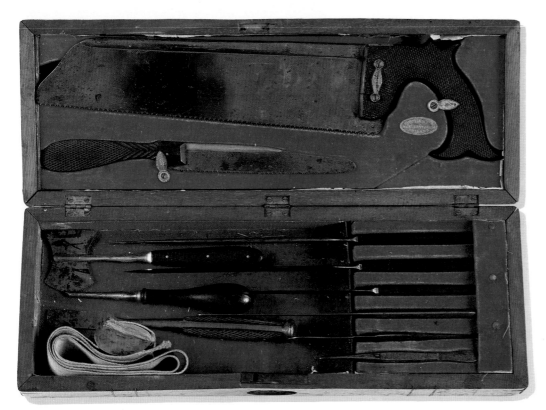

Many of the wounded who survived the battles spent the remainder of their lives in hospitals in and around Washington, D.C. (below, left). The medicine kits of the day included (clockwise from top, left) hacksaws for amputations; quinine for malaria; bullets for biting back the pain of opera-tions; pain-killing opium dispensed from bottles; blades used to induce bleeding; and syringes for injecting medicinal pow-ders into wounds.

tlefield their own portable darkrooms to chemically coat the plates before they were put into the giant camera. Then it was back again to the darkroom for immediate development after each picture was taken. The darkrooms were in special wagons nicknamed the ''What-is-it'' wagon since most soldiers couldn't conceive of what went on inside them.

The pictures of the war had a stunning effect on the civilians at home. It was the first time photography had delivered such shocking pictures of war's destruction and death. Oliver Wendell Holmes reported in the *Atlantic Monthly* after one battle:

> *These terrible mementoes of one of the most sanguinary conflicts of the war we owe to the enterprise of Mr. Brady of New York. . . . (We can see) the ditch encumbered with the dead. . . . Let him who wishes to know what war is, look at these series of illustrations. . . . It is so nearly like visiting the battlefields to look over these views . . . of the stained and sordid scene.*

The citizens of the 1860s were shocked to see realistic, grisly photos of the carnage. Stereoscopic pictures (right) show a rebel killed by artillery fire; he is barefoot as were many of the Confederate troops. The Battle of the Wilderness yielded many horrific views of the products of war (above, right) that enterprising photographers captured for posterity.

PHOTOGRAPHIC HISTORY

THE WAR FOR THE UNION

Entered according to Act of Congress in the year 1865, by E. & H.T. Anthony & Co. in the Clerk's Office of the District Court of the U.S. for the So.District of New York.

Unluckily for Brady, the war that brought him everlasting fame also made him bankrupt. By the end of the war, Brady owned a remarkable collection of photos of America's bloodiest conflict. But the American public was sick of bloodshed and was largely uninterested in viewing or buying pictures of the carnage. Brady was forced to put his plates into permanent storage.

When the battles ceased, Brady, who had spent all of his money outfitting himself and his assistants for their war reportage, resumed his portrait business, but his health and his finances never reached their prewar levels. He was still famous, but now there were other photographers who gave him plenty of competition.

After he died in 1896, most of his war photos stayed in storage for at least another ten years before historians rescued them and reconditioned as many as they could. But because of long neglect during storage, many of the plates had lost their images and a good number of these irreplaceable pictures were gone forever.

AFRICAN-AMERICANS IN THE CIVIL WAR

Was the Civil War fought to free the slaves? There is no satisfactory answer to this question. The war was ostensibly fought to preserve the Union, as Lincoln said time and time again.

While it is true that slavery seemed to be the most decisive issue separating the North and South, and that the slaves were certainly freed as a result of the conflict, it is also true, however, that most Northerners were just as racist as Southerners. Few whites at that time believed that any other race was equal to Caucasians. Even many abolitionists who advocated ending slavery didn't believe that, once they were freed, the Negroes were to be given equal citizenship. Maybe they wouldn't be slaves, but they wouldn't be much more than second-class citizens.

But if politics makes strange bedfellows, then the necessities of war makes odd comrades-in-arms. On November 7, 1864, President of the Confederacy Jefferson Davis said, "The slave bears another relation to the the State—that of a person." If African-Americans served in the army, he said, then the government should "liberate the Negro." These were the words of a man who knew that the South was losing the war and needed more men, even if those men were of a different color.

Lincoln, on the other hand, had issued his Emancipation Proclamation in September 1862, after the Union victory at Antietam. Even then, the Emancipation was only partial. Lincoln only freed the slaves in the Confederate states. Slaves living in states loyal to the Union were still in bondage. It wasn't until 1865 that these slaves were also freed and the "peculiar institution" of slavery was banished completely from the United States.

But the Emancipation Proclamation, which took effect in January 1863, had an important impact on the Union Army—it meant that the army could sign up African-Americans for combat roles. Up until this time, that had never happened. African-Americans had served as menials or laborers but had never been permitted to bear arms against the enemy.

Eventually, around 200,000 African-Americans carried rifles for the Union. Most of these men were former slaves, glad to have the chance to fight and destroy the Confederacy. But some units, such as the Fifty-fourth and Fifty-fifth Massachusetts, were made up of free African-Americans from the North.

While some whites disparaged the fighting ability of the "colored" units, their combat record soon showed that they could stand battle as well as white soldiers.

In one particularly well-known battle on July 18, 1863, an African-American unit under the command of Colonel Robert Gould Shaw (African-Americans always served under white officers) took part in a rather hopeless assault on Fort Wagner, Maryland. In the face of devastating artillery shelling, Shaw and his troops showed that African-Americans were heroically brave and loyal. In the attack, Shaw was killed and his unit was virtually wiped out as Confederate firepower tore them into scattered bits of flesh

At the beginning of the war, the Union resisted calls to use African-Americans as soldiers. When they were given the chance, however, black soldiers proved themselves as valorous as any other troop in the field. This unit is Company E, 4th U.S. Colored Infantry. The bugle emblem pictured on the hats (above) was an Infantry insignia.

During the Civil War, white officers always commanded African-American soldiers. Colonel Robert Gould Shaw headed the 54th Massachusetts, whose bravery at Fort Wagner, South Carolina, helped prove the dependability of black troops under fire. Shaw died in the attack. Confederates buried him in a mass grave with his troops.

and bones. Battles like this helped to allay Northern doubts about the courage of African-Americans under fire.

But the sight of former slaves in uniform upset Southerners greatly. And during the war, Confederates refused to take African-American prisoners. Instead, they killed all captured African-American soldiers in cold-blooded slaughter, as morally repugnant as the worst genocide of any war.

Perhaps the worst slaughter of African-American troops occurred at Fort Pillow, Tennessee, on April 12, 1864. In the aftermath of that battle, which was won by the Confederate cavalryman Nathan Bedford Forrest, both white and black prisoners were killed after they surrendered. Forrest is reported to have said that this encounter proved blacks couldn't hold their own as soldiers. Although Forrest was a military tactical genius (his simple philosophy was "get there first with the most"), he was a nasty character who had been a slave-trader before the war. Even though Southerners approved of slavery, they despised people like Forrest who made their living buying and selling human beings. After the war, Forrest is believed to have become the first head of the Ku Klux Klan.

When Union General William Tecumseh Sherman marched through the heart of the Confederacy in his famous march to the sea, he laid waste to everything in his path. To objections that his methods were too harsh, he replied, "War is cruelty and you cannot refine it." Opposite page: By the end of the war, the Union had taken its revenge on the rebelling Confederacy as these shots of ruins in Richmond, Virginia, the Confederate capitol, attest.

SHERMAN'S MARCH TO THE SEA AND THE END OF THE CONFEDERACY

As Grant carried on his war of attrition against Lee, General William Tecumseh Sherman skillfully applied some of the lessons the Union Army had learned during the campaign against Vicksburg. In its effort to destroy the South's resistance, he realized it wasn't necessary for the army to preserve its supply lines. The Union army could just as easily march through the heart of the South and live off the land at the same time as it rendered that land useless for the Confederacy.

Sherman captured Atlanta, Georgia, on September 2, 1864, and ordered the evacuation of all of Atlanta's civilian population. The locals protested that he was being too harsh. Sherman replied that he was doing what was necessary to win the war—make war against all of the enemy's citizens, not merely its soldiers. "War is cruelty and you cannot refine it," he said. Later, he was to point out in one of his most famous quotations, "War is hell."

Before he left Atlanta for his march to the sea, Sherman burned the town so the Confederates could not use it after he was gone. (It had been a major Southern railroad center.)

Sherman wasn't alone in his scorched-earth policy. At the same time, in the Shenandoah Valley of Virginia, Union General Philip Sheridan was burning down farms, railroad

then burned. Pianos were taken and broken up for kindling and wire. Irregular troops and hangers-on, called "bummers," traveled with Sherman's troops and treated the trip to the sea as one long party of looting and thievery.

Along the way, fleeing slaves flocked to Sherman's troops, following them down the road to freedom. So many freed slaves accompanied Sherman on his marches that at one point, as he met up with another Union outfit, he reported, "We bring in some five hundred prisoners and about ten miles of Negroes." And to the Southern argument that blacks actually preferred the stability of slavery to freedom, he asked, "Why, then, are so many of them glad to walk three hundred miles to escape?" In fact, it was reported that some African-American women carried their children 250 miles or more while following Sherman's troops to freedom.

When Sherman (below) marched into Georgia, he found that Atlanta was protected by substantial Confederate fortifications (opposite page). But Union control of the territory around the city starved the city's protectors into submission. And by the time both armies had finished destroying facilities like the Atlanta railroad depot (left), the city was a shambles.

stations, and granaries so that Lee would be hard pressed for supplies there, too.

But Sherman proved to be the master at causing devastation. As he marched, his army confiscated everything that could be carried away. Sherman noted, "We found abundance of corn, molasses, meal, bacon, and sweet potatoes. We also took a good many cows and oxen and a large number of mules. In all these, the country was quite rich, never before having been visited by a hostile enemy." But it wasn't rich after Sherman got through with it.

Feather beds were impressed for use in camp—and then slashed when camp was broken and the army moved on. Cotton bales were confiscated and used as mattresses and

The house in which Grant accepted Lee's final surrender, effectively ending the war, belonged to Wilmer McLean. At the beginning of the war, McLean and his family (right) had moved from their house in Manassas, site of the opening Battle of Bull Run, to the quiet town of Appomattox Court House to escape the war. Instead, it ended in their parlor.

THE WAR ENDS WITH A FEW MORE BANGS AND A WHIMPER

By the beginning of 1865, Sherman's devastating march to the sea, Grant's successes in battle, and Lee's steadily worsening position with desertions, casualties, sickness, and lack of supplies draining his army's fighting ability, spelled doom for the South.

Even the slave holders knew their days were numbered: despite the raging inflation in the Confederacy, the price of slaves had dropped by more than twenty percent since the start of the war. Desertion became such a major problem for the Southern armies that by the spring of 1865, many of its units were missing half of their men. A good many of these AWOLs had left to go back to farming. Their families were starving at home and they saw no point in getting killed in a lost cause.

In early April of 1865, the Confederates were forced to evacuate Richmond and surrender it to the Federals. In a supreme gesture of futility, the Confederates burned what few ships they had left in the harbor. In the subsequent conflagration, much of the town caught fire, the last fleeting hopes of the South going up in smoke along with the buildings.

With Lee's surrender, the war was essentially over. It had cost more than 610,000 American lives. At the end of the war, the Union, which had started with less than seventeen thousand soldiers, had more than a million men in uniform—the largest army in the world at the time.

Lee retreated to Appomattox Court House where, badly outnumbered and at the head of an army that was starving to death, he surrendered to Grant on Palm Sunday, April 9, 1865. During the next two months, the few other remaining Confederate armies surrendered one by one.

At Appomattox Court House, the tale of the Civil War ended. But five days later, John Wilkes Booth shot and killed Lincoln. In the shadow of Lincoln's murder, the tale of the reconstruction of the South had begun.

This ribbon commemorates Lieutenant Colonel Augustus Root, a Union soldier shot by Confederates the day before Lee surrendered. The Grand Army of the Republic Veteran's Post in Syracuse was named in his honor—Root Post #151.

After the war, Robert E. Lee served as the president of Washington College in Lexington, Virginia. Here he is shown a few days after surrendering to Grant. He died in 1870.

SOURCES

Beringer, Richard, et al. *Why the South Lost the Civil War.* Athens: University of Georgia Press, 1986.

Horan, James D. *Mathew Brady, Historian With a Camera.* New York: Crown, 1955.

Leckie, Robert. *None Died in Vain.* New York: HarperCollins, 1990.

Lewis, Lloyd. *Sherman, Fighting Prophet.* New York: Harcourt, Brace and World, 1960.

Sherman, W. T. *Memoirs.* New York: The Library of America, 1990.

Thomas, Emory. *The Confederate Nation.* New York: Harper and Row, 1979.

Ward, Geoffery C., et al. *The Civil War.* New York: Alfred A. Knopf, 1990.

Wheeler, Richard. *Voices of the Civil War.* New York: Thomas Y. Crowell, 1976.

Wiley, Bell Irvin. *They Who Fought Here.* New York: Macmillan, 1959.

INDEX